OAKLAND COMMUNITY COLLEGE

3 2355 00202713 4

DISCARD

D1249292

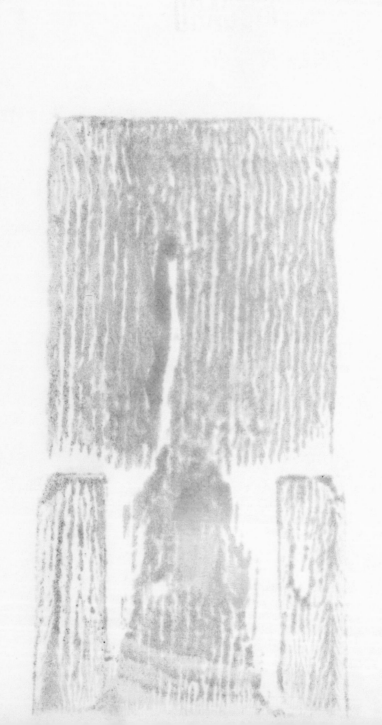

The Just War

ROBERT W. TUCKER

The

JUST

WAR

A Study in Contemporary

American Doctrine

THE JOHNS HOPKINS PRESS, BALTIMORE

© 1960 by The Johns Hopkins Press, Baltimore 18, Md.

Distributed in Great Britain by Oxford University Press, London

Printed in the United States of America by
Garamond Press, Baltimore, Maryland

Library of Congress Catalog Card Number 60-15755

This book has been brought to publication with the assistance
of a grant from the Ford Foundation.

To my Mother and Father

Acknowledgments

IT IS A PLEASANT DUTY TO ACKNOWLEDGE THE ASSISTANCE I received in writing this essay. My graduate students formed a group of perceptive critics and I was greatly benefited by their discussion of the problems considered in the following pages. Among them, Mr. Neil Folse assisted me ably in the editing of the text.

In the past year and a half I have been fortunate to participate in the weekly discussions of The Washington Center of Foreign Policy Research. These discussions, which encompass both the theoretical and practical problems of foreign policy, have provided me with an invaluable background, and I am very grateful to the members of the Center. The Center's director, Professor Arnold Wolfers, read the manuscript and gave me the benefit of his advice and criticism. In addition, his constant encouragement is recalled with gratitude. Above all, I must express my thanks to another member of the Center, Mr. James E. King, Jr. Whatever merit this essay may have is due in very large measure to the efforts of Mr. King. Through my frequent discussions with him were formed many of the ideas elaborated here. On more than one occasion, his penetrating insights provided the starting point for the development of problems I had not seen. It is difficult to record my full debt to this generous man and friend.

The Rockefeller Foundation facilitated the writing through a grant made in 1959.

Baltimore   *Robert W. Tucker*
July, 1960

Contents

The Just War

Introduction

I

ALTHOUGH IN THEIR SPECIFIC CONTENT THE JUSTIFICA-
tions which nations give when employing force vary end-
lessly, in their general structure these justifications nearly
always appear as variations on two central themes. Force is
justified as a means to the end of realizing some good that is
held to represent not only the interests of those who employ
this extreme form of coercion but the interests of a broader
community as well, a community that may even be extended
to embrace humanity as a whole. Or the employment of
force is seen as a necessity imposed upon the statesman and
the nation, a necessity variously attributed to religious, historic, or biological forces.

Thus the eternal human need to justify action, never
more apparent than when nations resort to force, has assumed
the form either of identifying a partial interest for which
force is most evidently and immediately employed with a
broader and perhaps universal interest or of placing the employment of force in the realm of necessity beyond the
statesman's power to alter or control. Not infrequently just
war doctrines have encompassed both claims, the difficulties
of their reconciliation being compensated for by an appeal
which gathers strength from its inclusiveness. Nations have
initiated wars while emphasizing the one claim, then have
gone on to wage those wars emphasizing the other claim.
The resort to war has occasionally been explained, and in
effect justified, simply in terms of the nation's instinctive

1

will-to-survive. But this justification has not precluded the concomitant claim that the nation's survival is an essential condition for the survival of values which represent the aspirations of all men. Nor has the justification of resorting to force by appeal to an instinctive will-to-survive prevented the later claim that the methods employed in war are justified by the purposes sought through war. Yet these purposes may bear no tangible relation to an instinctive will-to-survive. The complete defeat of an adversary and the demand for his unconditional surrender will rarely be required to satisfy an instinctive will-to-survive, though it may well be a necessary means for the realization of other purposes. But in the course of conflict nations have progressed from justifying that one purpose to justifying quite different purposes and whatever measures seemed designed to secure those varied purposes as though that progression were entirely natural and self-evident.

It is frequently assumed that the justifications nations urge when employing force are mere façades intended primarily to deceive others, that their principal function is to mask the true motives of action and the real interests sought through force, and that they have little if any influence on the actions of those who invoke them.[1] Even if this assumption were to

[1] Curiously enough, this assumption is often coupled with the rather contradictory argument that an obsession with justifying the employment of force can lead only to fanaticism and to punitive "wars for righteousness," and that this is particularly so when the nation pretends to act in terms of universal interests or in accordance with a moral law which it insists is equally valid for all nations. Whatever the merit of this argument, in all its variations it implicitly recognizes the significance for national conduct that may result from an insistence that the nation's behavior must be governed and the behavior of other nations judged by standards alleged to possess a universal validity. This significance may be deplored. It may be attributed to illusions that stem from a misunderstanding of the nature of state relations and particularly of the severe limitations held to condition and even to determine successful statecraft. Still, these very objections acknowledge that illusions may have important consequences for national behavior.

be accepted without qualification, these false fronts would
nevertheless remain significant and interesting as examples
of the manner in which men justify their behavior. But this
assumption surely cannot be accepted without substantial
qualifications. It is naïveté, not sophistication, to believe
that the convictions statesmen and nations profess and the
justifications they urge in defense of their actions have no
effect on the policies they pursue.

To be sure, the precise nature and extent of this influence
is extremely difficult to assess. Moreover, one of the chief
tasks of statecraft is to prevent a disparity between the act
and its justification from ever clearly arising. That task will
nearly always be facilitated by the complex character of the
circumstances in which the statesman is required to act, from
which comes also the ambiguity that inheres in their meaning. But while the ambiguity of circumstances is largely a
matter of chance, the ambiguity of the justification nations
urge in employing force is largely a matter of design, for the
more ambiguous the justification and the more vague the
principle on which it is alleged to rest, the less the possibility of any clear conflict with action. What must particularly give rise to skepticism in these matters, however, is not
the realization that justifications sufficiently ambiguous and
vague can always be somehow reconciled with action; instead
it is the further realization that even the justification that
appears to possess a clear meaning may nonetheless become
an instrument of diverse actions and serve quite disparate
national interests. One of the most striking and instructive
examples of this may be seen in doctrines which justify
force only as an act of self-defense.

Nevertheless, experience has shown that there is a point
beyond which the fine art of interpretation cannot easily go,
that in time the justification a nation professes in employing
force cannot always be altered to fit the shifting necessities
of policy, and that the disparity which may therefore arise

between justification and action cannot be readily obscured. Nor is this all. However spurious the particular justification for employing force, the purveyors of ideologies may not only believe their claims but may prove to be the most ardent believers. For the deepest roots of these claims are not to be found in the need to justify one's behavior to others or to deceive others, but to justify one's behavior to oneself. In the nature of things, this need for self-justification can only be satisfied by a varying degree of self-deception. It may be true that the most effective way to deceive others is first to deceive oneself. Even so, the possibility always remains that what men conceive to be their interests, and consequently the actions they take, will eventually be influenced by claims whose roots are found in this need for self-justification.

II

The intent of this essay is to inquire into the justification that has formed a part of the American response to the prospect of employing force in the nuclear age and to examine some of the dilemmas, moral and political, to which this prospect has given rise. The analysis undertaken in the following pages assumes that there is a publicly articulated doctrine dealing with the justification for employing force. The principal source of this doctrine may be found in the utterances of officials responsible for the conduct of foreign policy and entitled to speak for the nation. These expressions are not always identical in the views they suggest and the outlook they reflect. American statesmen have not spoken with one voice; nor have they justified policies pursued by invoking precisely the same catechism on every occasion. In style and outlook there have been obvious and at times even considerable differences. But these differences have seldom extended to what may be regarded as the essentials of doctrine. In the justification given for the employment of force—that is, the American just war doctrine—what has separated a Dean Acheson from a John Foster Dulles appears less significant than the framework of ideas and convictions that has been common to both.

In this analysis of the American just war doctrine no attempt has been made to provide an exhaustive inventory of statements and declarations made by American statesmen. The statements that have been cited are offered simply as illustrative material for points considered central to the doctrine. The question a discerning reader will raise is not whether these materials are illustrative of the points emphasized but whether the analysis when taken as a whole presents a reasonably true picture of the contemporary American justification for employing force. Unfortunately, the answer to this question will depend upon a judgment for which objective criteria are very largely lacking. But whatever the objection raised, it cannot be based simply on the grounds that the analysis is selective in its emphasis, for selectivity in these matters is inescapable.

To assume that there is a public doctrine respecting the justification for employing force is one thing. To assume further that this doctrine reflects the "moral consensus" of the nation as a whole is quite another matter. It is only to be expected that in addressing other nations the statesman will claim to speak in the name of a united nation and will insist that his voice is indeed the authentic voice of the nation. At best, this claim always contains an element of pretense, even for democratic societies. Indeed, the element of pretense involved may be greater in the case of democratic societies, since unity of view must normally be elicited and not imposed. Given sufficient opportunity to exercise its critical faculties, and the will to do so, a democratic society still rarely, if ever, achieves the degree of unity of outlook

in confronting the external adversary that totalitarian
societies not infrequently attain. Democratic statesmen, and
the theorists of democracy as well, have been loathe to
acknowledge this uncomfortable fact; they have seen fit to
argue that "real unity" and "true consensus" is only possible
when it springs from a consent that nevertheless remains
aware of alternatives and is free to consider these alternatives. But this argument cannot obscure the experience that
the methods of democracy may readily promote division
rather than unity in foreign policy and lead to indecision
rather than to resolution. No doubt, the conflict of opinion
and interest that democracy presupposes as normal and even
accepts as inevitable has not always proven a liability when
applied to the conduct of foreign policy. It is absurd to
argue, however, that the methods of democracy have in no
substantial way impeded the conduct of an effective foreign
policy. The benefits of democracy may be well worth the
price paid for them in the conduct of foreign policy. But
this is not to argue that these benefits entail no price.

At any rate, it is difficult to speak with assurance on the
extent to which the doctrine examined in these pages reflects
the consensus of the nation. What evidence there is of a
climate of public opinion on such complex and rather in-
tangible matters is almost always inconclusive. Even so, it
seems not unreasonable to assume that those individuals who
speak for the nation would not persist in the expression of
certain views unless they struck a fairly responsive chord
among the public. Democratic statesmen are not insensitive
to the prevailing public sentiment nor indifferent to that
sentiment. It is, for example, reasonably clear that the renunciation of force save as an act of self or collective defense
against aggression has formed an article of faith shared by
government and public alike. Similarly, the official condemnation of preventive war has quite obviously reflected a
widespread public sentiment. The extent to which the

official justification given the strategy of nuclear deterrence has met with public approval and satisfied the "public conscience" may be less clear. Still, the absence over the past decade of any widespread protest against even the more extreme versions of this strategy would seem to indicate that nuclear deterrence has offended the moral sensibilities of no more than a very small minority. Though the extent of this consensus on the justification for employing force should not be exaggerated, this note of caution does not imply that there is no consensus at all on these matters.

Too often inquiries of the kind attempted in these pages have been conducted almost in oblivion to military reality, with a result bordering on irrelevance. Throughout the present study an effort is made to avoid this unfortunate separation and to refrain from considering moral issues in a military vacuum. At the same time, a certain oversimplification of military reality is unavoidable, if only because the focus of the analysis is elsewhere. There is the further consideration that in dealing with almost any of the problems—moral, political, or military—raised by modern warfare a writer has the uncomfortable feeling that he is standing on shifting sands and that whatever he writes is very likely to appear dated all too soon. The natural response to this predicament is to seek a compromise between the concrete and specific, without which the relevance of the analysis is not readily apparent, and the general and abstract, without which the analysis may soon appear as no more than a tract for the day. There is always the hazard that in seeking this compromise the result will be to encompass the worst of both worlds. But that is a risk which must be taken.

One final word of admonition is necessary before terminating these introductory remarks. The following analysis does not pretend to resolve the problem of reconciling force and justice. Its purpose is rather to examine the manner in which others have sought to effect such a reconciliation and to illuminate some of the difficulties encountered as well as some of the illusions fostered. The reader intent on finding "solutions" to the moral dilemmas raised by the prospect of employing force in the nuclear age must therefore look elsewhere.

I

The American Doctrine
of the Just War

I

THERE IS AN APPARENT SIMPLICITY ABOUT the American doctrine of the just war that readily lends it to caricature. Undoubtedly the most striking characteristic of this doctrine is its simplicity. The American doctrine is distinguished by the assumption that the use of force is clearly governed by universally valid moral and legal standards; it is distinguished further by the insistence with which these standards are interpreted as making the justice or injustice of war primarily dependent upon the circumstances immediately attending the initiation of force. In substance, the just war is the war fought either in self-defense or in collective defense against an armed attack. Conversely, the unjust—and, of course, the unlawful[1]—war is the war initiated in circumstances other than those of self or collective defense against armed aggression.

This singular preoccupation with the overt act of resorting to force has its counterpart in the lack of concern shown toward the causes that have led to war; whatever the nature

---

[1] In American doctrine, the just war is also the lawful war, the *bellum justum* is equated with the *bellum legale*. International instruments to which we have subscribed, e.g., the Kellogg-Briand Pact and the Charter of the United Nations, are looked upon as legal expressions of the moral law. So also, the various security arrangements we have entered into since 1948 are seen as legal manifestations of the moral law.

of these causes, they cannot be regarded as providing a justification for the initiation of war. "We must make clear to
the Germans," Mr. Justice Jackson stated in 1945 in setting
forth the American position on the prosecution of German
leaders for having committed crimes against peace, "that
the wrong for which their fallen leaders are on trial is not
that they lost the war, but that they started it. And we must
not allow ourselves to be drawn into a trial of the causes
of war, for our position is that no grievances or policies will
justify resort to aggressive war."[2] And in his opening address
before the International Military Tribunal at Nuremberg,
the American prosecutor was even more explicit in declaring
that "Our position is that whatever grievances a nation may
have, however objectionable it finds that *status quo,* aggressive warfare is an illegal means for settling those grievances or
for altering those conditions."[3]

The insistence that whatever its grievances a state cannot
justify initiating war, that whatever its interests a state
should not resort to war to preserve or protect these interests,
stretches back through Roosevelt, Stimson, and Wilson and
surges forward through Truman, Acheson, Eisenhower, and
Dulles. "It is not necessary," Secretary Stimson wrote in
1932 on the outbreak of the Sino-Japanese conflict, "to
inquire into the causes of the controversy or attempt to appor-
tion the blame between the two nations which are unhappily
involved; for regardless of cause or responsibility, it is clear
beyond peradventure that a situation has developed which
cannot, under any circumstances, be reconciled with the obligations of the covenants of these two treaties, and that if the
treaties had been faithfully observed such a situation could

[2] Statement by Robert H. Jackson, Chief Counsel for the United States
in the Prosecution of Axis War Criminals, August 8, 1945 (*Department of
State Bulletin,* XII, 228; cited hereafter as *Bulletin*) .

[3] *Trial of Major War Criminals before the International Military Tribunal*
(1947), II, 149.

not have arisen."[4] A quarter of a century later, in condemning the resort to force by Great Britain, France, and Israel against Egypt, President Eisenhower declared that although "there have indeed been injustices suffered by all nations involved . . . I do not believe that another instrument of injustice—war—is the remedy for these wrongs."[5] In addressing the United Nations General Assembly on the Suez crisis, Secretary Dulles elaborated on this point in observing that "if we were to agree that the existence of injustice in the world, which this organization so far has been unable to cure, means that the principle of renunciation of force is no longer respected and that there still exists the right wherever a nation feels itself subject to injustice, to resort to force to try to correct that injustice, then . . . we would have, I fear, torn this Charter into shreds and the world would again be a world of anarchy."[6] The basic principle that must claim our allegiance and toward the realization of which we must

[4] Henry L. Stimson and McGeorge Bundy, On Active Service in Peace and War (1947), p. 254. The treaties referred to in the quotation are the Nine-Power Treaty of 1922 and the Kellogg-Briand Pact.

[5] Address to the Nation, October 31, 1956 (Bulletin, xxxv, 744-45).

[6] November 1, 1956 (Bulletin, xxxv, 752). Vice President Nixon contributed to the moral strictures that followed the Suez action by observing that if the United States had failed to stand by the principles of the United Nations, "Our position in the eyes of most of the world would have been little better than that of the Communist nations who in their conduct of international affairs have consistently followed the principles that the end justifies the means, that the use of force is justified if it is expedient, and that the mandates of the United Nations are to be followed only where the nation affected concludes that its national interest will be served thereby." Address to the Automobile Manufacturers Assn., New York, December 6, 1956 (Bulletin, xxxv, 944). Perhaps the most remarkable statement on the Suez episode, however, came from Walter Robertson, the Assistant Secretary for Far Eastern Affairs. "That the situation was tragic I would be the last to deny, but to say that what we did was wrong is to misconstrue entirely the nature of the conflict that has so largely preoccupied us during the past decade. We have not fought and toiled to establish the rule of any particular set of nations in the world; we have done so to establish the rule of certain principles embodied in the Charter of the United Nations which we believe

constantly strive is that of banishing force as an instrument of national policy. The realization of this principle would presumably be jeopardized were we once to
concede even the partial identification of the justice of war
with the causes that ultimately led to the initiation of force.

War then becomes in this doctrine an "instrument of
national policy" not primarily for the reason that it serves
to further the interests of a particular nation, but presumably
because it is initiated in circumstances not sanctioned by the
international society. When war is undertaken in conformity
with the standards allegedly sanctioned by this society, it
must be regarded as an "instrument of international policy."
Thus a war waged in self or collective defense against armed
aggression becomes an instrument of international policy,
even though such a war may also serve to advance distinctly
national interests.

It is apparent, of course, that this doctrine, if consistently
followed, must lead to the absolute condemnation of a policy
of so-called preventive war. From the technical military
standpoint, a preventive war is an aggressive war only in that
it implies the initiation of armed hostilities—striking the
first blow. From the political point of view, a preventive
war has for its purpose, as the term indicates, the prevention
of what is regarded as the otherwise probable sacrifice of
some vital interest of the nation, which is thought to be pre-
ventable only through the aggressive resort to force at the
most propitious moment. The moral justification for preventive war must be found, if at all, in the nature of the
interests a state seeks to defend through waging aggressive
war, in the scope and gravity of the threat posed to these

are entitled to universal respect. Any state that honors and defends these
principles—the chief of which is that no state should attack another—is our
ally. Any state violating them, even under painful provocation, will find us
in opposition concerning these issues regardless of how long and close our
association has been. Address to the University of Virginia, Charlottesville,
Va., April 13, 1957 (*Bulletin*, xxvii, 686).

interests, and in the consequences that may not unreasonably be expected to follow from the resort to force. And this must necessitate relating the justice of preventive war, in turn, to the causes of war, to the specific objectives sought in employing force, and to the manner of employing force.

It would hardly seem necessary to point out that even given the most favorable and the least ambiguous circumstances there are serious moral objections which can be raised against a policy of preventive war. Yet, apart from a purely pacifist position, preventive war as a possible instrument of policy cannot be excluded on moral grounds alone save by a doctrine which insists upon identifying the justice or injustice of war with the acts immediately attending the initiation of force. For this doctrine preventive war is not only aggressive war in the technical military sense; it is also aggressive war in the moral sense and as such unjust. Because preventive war implies condoning the resort to war by a state in circumstances other than those of self or collective defense against armed aggression, it signifies the acceptance of war as an instrument of national rather than of international policy. Preventive war must therefore be condemned, whatever the circumstances that are alleged to condition its initiation and however unambiguous these circumstances may appear. Thus President Truman in setting forth the aims of American policy during the Korean conflict declared: "We do not believe in aggressive or preventive war. Such war is the weapon of dictators, not of free democratic countries." [7] The very idea of preventive war, in the words of Dean Acheson, "is a thoroughly wicked thing . . . immoral and wrong from every point of view." [8] Nor is this position shaken by the conviction that the adversary is dedicated to crushing us, and that he will not be inhibited in using every means for bringing about this end.

[7] Address to the Nation, September 1, 1950 (*Bulletin*, xxiii[1], 409).
[8] Television interview, September 10, 1950 (*Bulletin*, xxiii[1], 460).

"We shall never choose a war as the instrument of our policy," John Foster Dulles declared repeatedly as Secretary of State, even though "we know that our enemies do not have moral scruples. In fact, they deny that there is such a thing as moral law." [9]

Whatever the logical consistency of this position, the evidence available is impressive in pointing to the significance of moral conviction in rejecting the possibility of preventive war by those who nevertheless remained convinced of the complete moral depravity of the adversary and of his fanatic commitment to a deeply hostile philosophy. To be sure, as a problem for American policy, preventive war cannot be divorced from the actual political and military circumstances in which it has had to be considered. Nevertheless, it is not obvious that these circumstances have been uniformly unfavorable to the successful execution of such a policy.

The argument that at no time since the inception of Soviet-American rivalry have circumstances offered a promise of success to a policy of preventive war appears strained. It must assume that at best the United States never attained more than an over-all position of equality with the Soviet Union in terms of a military capability for waging general war, and that at no time could a Soviet-American conflict have resulted in anything better than a military standoff in which both sides would emerge in approximately the same power position as before. If this argument were to be accepted as substantially correct, then the American position has been hopeless from the very start. But what of the period, for example, extending from the closing stages of the Korean conflict to approximately the spring of 1955—a period of between two to three years? While still markedly inferior in conventional forces to the Soviet Union, the United States

[9] Address to the Nation, January 27, 1953 (*Bulletin*, xxviii, 215).

had reached a point at which its strength in conventional forces—supplemented by the forces of its European allies—was not inconsiderable. The decisive point, however, is that it was during this period that America clearly achieved a position of nuclear "abundance" and the means of efficient delivery, whereas the Soviet Union was still wanting in both.[10]

It is also true that the idea of preventive war must prove offensive to this nation if only for the reason that it implies (or, at least, it has been uniformly interpreted as implying) the notion of war's inevitability. As will presently be noted, that notion runs directly counter to the American interpretation of conflict. Perhaps of equal significance in the rejection of preventive war has been the belief that "time is on our side," and this being so it would be not only immoral but stupid to choose a policy of preventive war. "The basic premise of our foreign policy," Secretary Acheson pointed out in the 1951 Senate hearings on the dismissal of General MacArthur, "is that time is on our side if we make good use of it."[11] Even the qualification implicit in this statement was to disappear in the confident assertions of Mr. Acheson's successor. "The working hypothesis on which we conduct our foreign policy," Secretary Dulles declared six years later

[10] In these circumstances a former Chairman of the Atomic Energy Commission, looking ahead to a time when the Soviets would acquire a position of nuclear parity, could write: "Can we as a nation and can the now free world permit the Soviet to reach this position of power? For reach it she will; and all the fervent hopes of free people everywhere will not deny her this terrible capability unless those hopes are reduced to action of some sort which forces open the Iron Curtain and brings a halt to her enormous weapons program. . . . This, very bluntly, is the very great problem of 1953-1954." Gordon Dean, "Tasks for the Statesmen," *Bulletin of Atomic Scientists,* January, 1954, p. 11.

[11] Hearings before the Joint Senate Committee on Armed Services and Committee on Foreign Relations, *Military Situation in the Far East* (82nd Cong., 1st Sess.) , Part III, p. 1720.

in 1957, "is that free governments in the long run are going to prevail and despotic governments in the long run are going to go under." [12]

Thus the transient character of the Soviet and Chinese regimes is guaranteed simply because they are evil, because they do not recognize the "moral law," because they have, as President Truman pointed out in his farewell address to the American nation, "a fatal flaw in their society." It is not war then that is ever inevitable in history, but only the victory of the moral law—of good over evil. And this confidence in the inevitable triumph of good over evil, hence of this nation over its adversaries, has always been supported—at least until very recently—by an equal confidence in the inevitability of our material superiority, a superiority that is itself interpreted as being largely the consequence of our moral superiority.

The foregoing remarks ought not to be interpreted therefore as suggesting that in the rejection of a policy of preventive war factors other than moral conviction have been without importance. They do suggest that it would be rash to discount the significance of "pure" moral conviction in this matter.

II

Every nation is disposed to interpret the world in the light of the interpretation it has given to its domestic experience. America has been no exception to this pattern. Our interpretation of the world beyond our borders is clearly a reflection of the interpretation we have given to our own rise and development as a nation. The freedom we find in our own historical development has been transformed into

[12] News Conference, July 2, 1957 (*Bulletin*, xxxvii, 143).

a general view of history from which it would seem unreasonable to exclude international political history, and consequently the history of international conflict. Although the American interpretation of international conflict is to be distinguished for a number of reasons from the interpretation of conflict implicit in the classic continental doctrine of "reason of state," there is perhaps no reason more striking than the voluntarism assumed by the former and the determinism informing the latter. In the doctrine of *raison d'état,* war appears much more a matter of necessity than of choice, and the justice of resorting to war is deduced from its necessity, that is, from the "natural" and consequently the necessary power imperatives of the state, which must secure its existence in an environment of potentially hostile states. In the American interpretation, it is almost as though this sequence were reversed and the necessity of war deduced from principle, that is, from the moral law whose universal validity has always been assumed as an article of faith. Viewed through the prism of the American interpretation of conflict, the doctrine of *raison d'état* appears esoteric and obscure in its interpretation of conflict and morally perverse in its justification for resorting to war.[13]

[13] Since the significance of the distinction between the justification given for war in the doctrine of *raison d'état* and the justification given for war in the prevailing American doctrine is still frequently misunderstood, a few general remarks seem necessary. One of the critical problems posed by the doctrine of *raison d'état* concerns the conflict that arises between two principles in the conduct of statecraft—the one principle postulating the state, its security and independence (though perhaps much more as well), as the highest value, the other principle postulating certain norms (respect for human life, fidelity to obligations, etc.) which cannot be identified simply with the security and independence of the state and the observance of which may even conflict with these ends. The difference between the justification given for the resort to war in the doctrine of *raison d'état* and the justification for war in the American concept of the just war cannot be based on the assertion that whereas the former accepts the moral supremacy of state security and independence, the latter consciously accepts the supremacy of norms whose observance may endanger the state's security or independence.

To be sure, our well-known insistence that it is the aggressor who has the "choice" of war or peace, whereas we have no choice when resorting to war but must act under "necessity," may seem to contradict the contrast drawn above. Yet, if properly understood, it confirms rather than contradicts the substance of this contrast. For the meaning of our insistence is that the aggressor has the choice of war or peace in the sense that he is not bound by moral principle, not "compelled" by the moral law. We do not have the same choice, however, because we must presumably act in conformity with the moral law. Hence, the "necessity" under which we act is the "necessity of principle." And this is

Even the most congenital ideologue would be hard put to support this assertion in a period that has witnessed the enthusiastic acceptance—political and moral—of a policy of deterring any aggression affecting our national security by the threat of massive nuclear retaliation. But there is a significant difference in that *raison d'état* assumes that action required by the moral imperative of state security and independence will not always and necessarily coincide with the action required by other moral principles, and that when a choice has to be made—e.g., in resorting to war—it must be for the state. The American doctrine does not admit the possibility of this divergence, however, since it has assumed that the necessity for resorting to war can always be deduced from or will coincide with those allegedly universal moral principles to which allegiance is professed. It is evident that the difference here is one which concerns the interpretation of the nature of state relations in general and in particular the necessities held to govern a successful statecraft, and not a difference over the value to be assigned the security and independence of the state. On the other hand, it is quite true that the doctrine of *raison d'état* has always been obscure with respect to the moral justification of action clearly exceeding the requirements of security and independence and calculated simply to extend the power of the state. This obscurantism has brought forth the charge that the doctrine of *raison d'état* in reality accepts the moral supremacy of a standard which postulates that the actions of the state ought only to be limited by the power the state has at its disposal. Thus an action will be immoral when it results in a loss of security for the state or when it jeopardizes the very independence of the state. But as long as these consequences are avoided the action may be morally approved. Hence, the successful expansion of power joins security and independence as the highest moral imperative for the statesman—and for the citizen. Clearly, the American doctrine must be distinguished from *raison d'état* on this significant point.

the significance of the phrase "deducing necessity from principle" in describing the American interpretation of international conflict. Of course, from the point of view of a historical interpretation of conflict—and, particularly, when juxtaposed with the interpretation of conflict implicit in the doctrine of *raison d'état*—the American doctrine does not presuppose "necessity," but "freedom."

It is this marked voluntarism in our interpretation of conflict, and not simply a moral aversion to violence, that has given a distinctive character to the American doctrine of the just war. A general moral aversion to resolving the conflicts of interest that arise among nations by the resort to armed force is not unique to this nation. Other nations share this sentiment, despite our rather prideful assumption that we are perhaps history's most shining example of a nation of true peacemakers. Besides, the depth of our aversion to violence must be suspect if only because of the curious ambivalence with which we have viewed, and with which we continue to view, the instrument of force. An extreme reluctance to resort to war has not implied restraint in the manner of employing force once war has been thrust upon us. This lack of restraint that we have shown in conducting war—and the lack of restraint with which we have threatened to conduct war should it once again be imposed upon us—has commonly been attributed to the indignation we feel toward the "aggressor" who initially resorted to armed force.[14] Nevertheless, the explanation of our behavior by its reference to retributive motives does not resolve the moral ambiguities of that

[14] Thus in the first official statement following the dropping of an atomic bomb on Hiroshima, President Truman declared: "Having found the bomb, we have to use it. We have used it against those who attacked us without warning at Pearl Harbor, against those who have starved and beaten and executed American prisoners of war, against those who have abandoned all pretense of obeying international laws of warfare. We have used it in order

behavior. Still less does it show how that behavior can be reconciled with an allegedly profound moral aversion to the methods of violence.

More serious, perhaps, is the consideration that a profound moral aversion to violence cannot readily be reconciled with a view that war, even a just war, may serve as the means for bringing untold blessings to the world. Yet once we have entered upon war, there have been few nations more disposed to believe that history can be radically transformed for the better through the instrument of unrestrained violence.[15] And in the nuclear age this belief has found its expression in a philosophy of deterrence which optimistically assumes that history can be radically transformed for the better simply by confronting would-be aggressors with the certainty of severe punishment in the form of nuclear retaliation should they seek to carry out their evil designs.

to shorten the agony of war, in order to save the lives of thousands and thousands of young Americans." Address to the Nation, August 9, 1945 (*Bulletin*, XIII, 212-13). The order of presentation of the reasons given for using the bomb is perhaps as significant as the reasons themselves.

[15] In reflecting on the American attitude toward war Robert Osgood points out that "if moral sensibilities forbid the use of war as an instrument of national policy, they do not prevent the use of war as an instrument of ideology, once war has become unavoidable. In a sense they encourage this; for tender consciences find in broader, more exalted goals a kind of moral compensation for the enormity of war and a rational justification for their contamination with evil. Thus the very ideals that proscribe war become the incentive for fighting war. An aversion to violence is transmuted into the exaltation of violence." *Limited War* (1957), p. 33. Paul Kecskemeti, in his study of strategic surrender during World War II, speaks of the American assumption that there is "a causal connection between maximum destructiveness in war and the perpetual peace that is to succeed it." *Strategic Surrender* (1958), p. 167. The Korean war may be cited as a rather obvious exception to these remarks. The exception is not so obvious, however. The widespread equation of our restraint in conducting the Korean hostilities with what were regarded as the meager and disappointing results of that war may not have strengthened the view that once in war history can be transformed for the better through the instrument of unrestrained violence, but it would surely be rash to assert that the Korean experience seriously challenged this view.

Neither view would appear particularly appropriate for achieving the purpose of reducing the influence of force in history. If war, once entered into, is conceived as offering such grandiose possibilities, then the role force must play in determining the destinies of nations has not been reduced but inordinately increased. It may be less apparent, however, that if the threat of nuclear war is presently conceived as holding forth equally grandiose possibilities, the mere specter of such a war may prove sufficient to dominate the course of future history in a way that war itself could never do in the past. The ironic result of banishing the actuality of force from history might nevertheless be to give to force an importance it had never before possessed.

At any rate, a simple moral aversion to violence cannot alone adequately account for the fervor with which we have condemned the recourse to war as an instrument of national policy and the intense moral indignation with which we have looked upon aggressor states. That fervor and indignation stem not only from the belief that war as such is an evil but also from the belief that its initiation is an unnecessary evil. It is quite true that this same belief extends as well to forms of conflict which fall short of armed force. The American vision of an international order characterized by co-operation rather than conflict, and based upon the principles of equality and consent rather than hierarchy and coercion, is not simply held out as an ideal to be striven after though perhaps never attained in reality. On the contrary, the ideal is considered the "natural" condition, and the antagonisms and conflicts among nations are viewed as a departure from what must be regarded the normal state of affairs. Thus Walter Lippmann has written of our "refusal to recognize, to admit, to take as the premise of our thinking, the fact that rivalry and strife and conflict among states, communities, and factions are the normal condition of mankind. . . . In the American ideology the struggle for existence, and the rivalry for advantages, are held to be wrong, abnormal, and transitory. . . ."[16] But although the American concept of international order is assumed as imminent, in the sense that the intrinsic justice of the principles upon which it is based are regarded as self-evident, the realization of this order obviously remains an aspiration, not a fact. In the world as it is, conflict and antagonism are acknowledged, however reluctantly. Nevertheless, the distinction that is drawn between conflict carried on by methods which fall short of armed force and conflict pursued by armed force remains, and this is the significant point.

The relations among states may continue to be marked by antagonisms and conflicting interests, but the use of force is not regarded as simply one method among a number that either ought or need to be employed to secure a nation's interests or to resolve favorably the conflicts in which it is engaged. The critical distinction that is drawn between "peaceful" methods of diplomacy and methods involving the employment of force does not have a purely normative significance therefore, and the tenacity with which this distinction is held cannot be attributed simply to the strength of moral conviction. This distinction can be fully appreciated only in the light of the belief that whatever other necessities are imposed upon nations in order to insure their security and independence, let alone to preserve their other interests, the initiation of force is not one of them. The idea of preventive war, in suggesting the heresy that war may well be in certain circumstances a necessary evil, appears doubly offensive then. Apart from its intrinsic immorality, it implies the notion of war's inevitability. It is the "utter fallacy" of this notion that American statesmen have been at such pains to expose. There simply "is no such thing as an inevitable war," in the words of General Brad-

16 "The Rivalry of Nations," *The Atlantic Monthly*, February, 1948, p. 18.

ley.[17] It is "talk about war being inevitable which tends to make it so," Secretary Acheson cautioned during the Korean war.[18]

When aggression occurs, therefore, it must be seen as an unnecessary act, as something that could easily have been avoided given only the will to do so. War cannot be the "choice of those who wish passionately for peace," General Marshall stated in his final report as Chief of Staff in 1945, "it is the choice of those who are willing to resort to violence for political advantage."[19] The aggressor not only wants to obtain things that others will not accord him, but wants things that he does not really "need"—at least, not at the price of deliberately choosing war as the instrument of national policy. Since there is nothing we have "needed" that could not be obtained by peaceful means, we have assumed that the same should and must hold true for other nations as well.[20] And if the conditions out of which aggres-

[17] Remarks made at Palm Beach roundtable on "War or Peace," March 2, 1953 (*Bulletin*, xxviii, 412).

[18] Television Interview, September 10, 1950 (*Bulletin*, xxiii, 460).

[19] Biennial Report of the Chief of Staff of the United States Army, July 1, 1943-June 30, 1945 in *The War Reports* (1947), p. 299.

[20] Perhaps more accurately, there is nothing we have needed in this century which could not be obtained by peaceful means if only other nations would refrain from employing force as an instrument of policy. One need not deny the importance of moral conviction to see in our attitude a convenient and useful rationalization for a nation possessing an economic superiority over its competitors. Given this superiority, a world in which the competition and rivalry of nations was restricted to means falling short of force would be a world in which America would possess a marked advantage. Whatever the exaggerations of William A. Williams' *The Tragedy of American Diplomacy* (1959) in identifying American policy since the turn of the century as the policy of the Open Door, and in defining the latter as an attempt "to establish the conditions under which America's preponderant economic power would extend the American system throughout the world without the embarrassment and inefficiency of traditional colonialism" (p. 37), it would be futile to deny the very important insight in his contention. Thus when other nations have resorted to force they have not only transgressed the requirements of the moral law, but they have discarded

sion or the threat of aggression emerges are not seen as
providing any plausible justification for this act, if the act
of resorting to aggression seems to bear no reasonable relation to the circumstances out of which it suddenly springs,
the aggressor's behavior not only must fall beyond the pale
of the moral law but must appear almost incomprehensible.
Thus there is the tendency—most fully developed in the
thought and words of Secretary Dulles—to view the aggressor
not only as willful and immoral but as a kind of "moral
idiot" whose behavior is little short of pathological.

The conviction that the resort to armed force is a wholly
unnecessary evil is also a significant factor in explaining the
insistence with which we identify the aggressor as no more
than an "evil few" and the care with which we distinguish
between these evil few and the great majority of innocent,
though perhaps temporarily misled, people. To be sure,
this distinction between the evil few and the many good
has other and still deeper roots. But it is essential to
a doctrine that persists in viewing armed conflict as an
entirely avoidable feature of history and one that has been
needlessly imposed upon men and nations. "One fact stands
out stark and clear," President Eisenhower has declared
in articulating this distinction. "Of all who inhabit the globe,
only relatively small numbers—only a handful even in Russia
itself—are fixed in their determination to dominate the
world by force and fraud. Except for these groups in the

those ground rules of competition the observance of which have conferred
upon this nation a substantial advantage. Our moral outrage toward the
aggressor reflects in some measure then the irritation we feel, however unconsciously, toward those who would attempt to deprive us of our "natural"
advantage. Of course, other nations have frequently viewed this happy
coincidence of the requirements of the moral law with the satisfaction of
American "needs" as mere hypocrisy. The oversimplification this judgment
reflects can be appreciated only when—as at present—that coincidence is
no longer so apparent, yet the "needs" of policy remain unfulfilled in order
to conform to the requirements of the moral law.

several nations . . . mankind everywhere hungers for freedom, for well-being, for peace." [21]

One might expect, not unreasonably, that this picture of a world divided into the evil few and the many good would give rise to a heightened sense of the tragedy involved in modern international conflict. Of course, all group conflict may be interpreted as tragic, if only because the very nature of collective strife necessarily involves the innocent along with the guilty. But this inevitable feature of collective strife is nevertheless a matter of degree, and that degree has provided one of the principal criteria, both political and moral, for distinguishing the character of group conflicts. With an interpretation of conflict that places so strong an emphasis upon severely limiting the identification of the "aggressor," it is only to be expected that a supreme effort will be made to conduct war so as to effect a meaningful distinction between the few judged responsible for aggression and the many whose responsibility can be assessed on no other basis than the fact of their membership in the aggressor state. It may well be that in view of the weapons and methods of warfare, and the "necessity" that is alleged to inhere in the latter, this effort will nevertheless prove to be without results, and in terms of the actual conduct of war the innocent will be equated with the guilty. Even so, the identification in modern warfare of the innocent with the guilty—however inevitable such identification is made to appear—might be expected to give rise to a profound feeling of unease and a deep sense of the tragedy such conflict must involve.

Yet what is apparent in the American interpretation of conflict is not a heightened sense of tragedy arising from the awareness of the gulf which separates aspiration from reality. Instead, one finds an optimism which springs from the as-

[21] Address at Columbia University, May 31, 1954 (*Bulletin,* xxx, 900).

sumption that the task of preventing aggression and securing peace in the international society forms a close parallel to this same problem as it has appeared within domestic society. In either case, the forces of aggression constitute no more than a small minority when compared with the community of peace-loving people. In both cases, the conditions out of which aggression emerges are substantially the same. Aggression occurs because aggressors miscalculate the determination and strength of those who ultimately will be ranged against them. And aggressors are tempted to miscalculate because peace-loving peoples all too frequently do not have the fortitude and the foresight to make clear their determination to resist aggression and the capacity with which to impress potential aggressors with the consequences that must be expected should the latter take the path of violence.

Thus to President Truman the victory of the rule of law and of order in the international society obviously imposed the same tasks upon us as the problems we once confronted in achieving law and order during the early days of our Western frontier when outlaws terrorized entire communities. "Men who wanted to see law and order prevail had to combine against the outlaws. . . . This is just what we are trying to do today in the international field."[22] How is it possible, asks President Eisenhower, for a "few men to thwart the will of hundreds of millions?"[23] Obviously it is possible because the former are well organized to impose their evil designs, whereas the latter have not had the will nor the capacity nor the organization to resist. One of the great advances of our time, therefore, is the recognition that "one of the ways to prevent war is to deter it by having the will and the capacity to use force to punish an aggressor." In

[22] Address at dedication of Chapel of the Four Chaplains, Philadelphia, February 3, 1951 (*Bulletin*, xxiv[1], 283).

[23] See note 21 above.

the thought of Secretary Dulles the recurring analogy drawn between the problems of domestic and the problems of international order reached its most articulate form. The prevention of aggression, Mr. Dulles declared on many occasions, "involves an effort, within the society of nations, to apply the principle used to deter violence within a community. There, laws are adopted which define crimes and their punishment. A police force is established, and a judicial system. Thus there is created a powerful deterrent to crimes of violence. This principle of deterrence does not operate 100 percent even in the best ordered communities. But the principle is conceded to be effective, and it can usefully be extended into the society of nations. That, as we have seen, has actually occurred in an impressive measure."[24]

Given this parallel between the repression of violence within domestic society and the repression of aggression in the international society, the conclusion naturally seems to follow that the circumstances in which force should be resorted to and need be resorted to for preserving order are in both cases substantially identical. Indeed, it would be surprising if this projection onto the international level of an interpretation of domestic experience were to lead to any other conclusion. And since the international society must exorcise aggression by following the same method employed in the repression of violence within domestic society, force is considered to be a function of international order in the same sense that it is a function of domestic order. Force must be used or threatened to prevent the aggressive use of force. But for "antisocial" behavior which falls short of the aggressive use of force, society, domestic and international, ought to and can effectively employ other means for preserving order and safeguarding the legitimate interests of its component parts.

[24] John F. Dulles, *War or Peace* (1957 ed.) , Foreword.

III

Although the American doctrine insists that the moral law requires the renunciation of force as an instrument of national policy, it does not thereby admit to a concept of international order in which peace, conceived simply as the absence of armed force, may be founded upon injustice. We want peace, but at the same time we have insisted that is must be a peace based upon justice. This insistence has been articulated in a number of ways. In Secretary Acheson's thought, justice was held to be a necessary ingredient of peace, and the two were considered as one. Peace, Mr. Acheson declared, "is not just the absence of war." The peace we strive for must be one in which we and the other peoples of the world are "free from fear" and "free from want." It must be a "moral peace."[25] To Secretary Dulles, justice formed the indispensable concomitant of peace, and the two were conceived to stand in a necessary relationship to each other. In one of his celebrated and most frequently invoked metaphors, Mr. Dulles expressed this point by comparing peace to "a coin which has two sides. One side is the renunciation of force, the other side is the according of justice. Peace and justice are inseparable."[26]

These statements need not be taken literally. The contention that there cannot be peace—conceived simply as the absence of force—unless there is justice as well is obviously untrue and does not merit serious consideration. Has history never known of an unjust peace? Insistence on the interdependence of peace and justice may be understood merely to express the truism that any peace must prove precarious if it is based upon a high degree of dissatisfaction

[25] Address to United Nations General Assembly, September 20, 1950 (*Bulletin,* xxiii[2], 529).

[26] John F. Dulles, *War or Peace* (1957 ed.), Foreword.

with the *status quo,* particularly on the part of nations possessing substantial power, and if no means other than force exists to alter the *status quo.* Peace may also prove precarious, however, if the established rights of nations may be violated and there is no effective way to obtain redress save by the resort to force. "If you have a world in which force is not used," Secretary Dulles insisted at an early stage of the crisis provoked by the nationalization of the Suez Canal, "you must also have a world in which a just solution of problems of this sort can be achieved. I don't care how many words are written into the Charter of the United Nations about not using force. If, in fact, there is not, as a substitute for force, some way to get just solutions of some of these problems, inevitably the world will fall back into anarchy and chaos." [27]

Nor has the adherence to the American doctrine of the just war been taken to imply the acceptance of an international system in which our security and the security of other nations is conceived only in terms of protection against the open and direct use of armed force. To be sure, we

[27] Remarks to 2nd Plenary Session on Suez Canal, London, September 19, 1956 (*Bulletin,* xxxv, 505). The Suez crisis was therefore held up as a clear illustration of the interdependence of peace and justice. Since the Canal was a "lifeline" for many nations, the attempt to exert exclusive control over it would require dependent nations "to live under an economic 'sword of Damocles.'" To be sure, the sentiment against using force to alter the situation created by the Egyptian seizure was described as "natural and proper." But, Secretary Dulles cautioned, "those who are concerned about peace ought to be equally concerned about justice. Is it just, or even tolerable, that great nations which have rights under the 1888 treaty and whose economies depend upon the use of the canal should accept an exclusive control of this international waterway by a government which professes to be bitterly hostile?" Address at Williams College, October 6, 1956 (*Bulletin,* xxxv, 573). Nevertheless, it is one thing to assert that the proscription on resorting to force will most likely remain ineffective if other means are not found to remedy injustice. It is quite another matter to assert that in such circumstances the proscription of force ought to fail. If nothing else, Secretary Dulles' condemnation of the Suez intervention was at least consistent with the views he expressed prior to the intervention.

want an international order in which we, along with other nations, will enjoy security against overt armed aggression. But we have been equally clear that the security we desire and indeed insist upon cannot be so limited. Obviously, the threat to a nation's security or independence need not arise merely from the open violation of its territorial integrity by the armed forces of another state. The American concept of security may not be a fountain of political wisdom, but it cannot seriously be charged with having been blind to perhaps the most significant and certainly the most frequent experience of a decade and a half. With the exception of Korea, all of the major crises marking American policy in the post-World War II period have been brought on by situations in which it has been contended that the security or independence of nations was threatened by methods other than the open violation of territorial integrity. And were it not for the exception of Korea, there would not be a single instance during this period in which the United States has contemplated the employment of force in response to what could be unambiguously characterized as an overt armed attack across a recognized international frontier.

Hence, the American concept of international order cannot be described as one in which peace is consciously conceived as a value both discrete from and higher than justice; nor is security considered simply in terms of protection against the overt resort to armed aggression. Nevertheless the question remains whether a just war doctrine that so narrowly circumscribes the occasions in which force may be resorted to will not in practice lead to conceiving peace and security in these terms. Justice may be regarded as an essential concomitant of peace. Yet the critical question in this context is whether the resort to force may be judged to have a moral sanction if there is no effective alternative method for securing justice. Or is force necessarily to be regarded as an instrument of injustice when resorted to aggressively, even though such resort appears at the time as the only effective reaction against a prior injustice? A literal reading of the American just war doctrine must answer the former question negatively and the latter question affirmatively. It is true that a literal reading of the American just war doctrine allows the conclusion that force may still be regarded as an instrument of order. But in view of the disparity arising between the circumstances in which doctrine sanctions the employment of force and the actual circumstances in which a nation's security may be threatened, force can be regarded as an instrument of order only in a severely restricted sense.

Of course, the condemnation of force as an instrument of national policy may be related primarily to the consequences that a war involving nuclear powers is assumed to entail. It may be argued that whatever the injustices suffered by a nation and however grave the threat to its security, the initiation of force must be morally condemned in view of the danger that any employment of force in the nuclear age may eventuate in a common catastrophe. Whatever merit this particular argument may possess must evidently depend upon the validity of the assumption which forms its basis, that is, the assumption of a strong possibility that any resort to force which directly or indirectly involves nuclear powers will lead to an unrestricted nuclear conflict. If this assumption is once accepted, the conclusion is unavoidable that force may no longer serve as an instrument of order, that the disorder created by the resort to force must prove greater than the disorder to be corrected by the employment of force. Even so, the distinctly moral judgment that may be drawn from this assumption—that force can no longer serve as an instrument of justice since the injustice force must give rise to is greater than the injustice it seeks to remedy—

cannot prove compelling.[28] At any rate, the question of its acceptance or rejection is not at issue here. Of relevance here is only the influence this reasoning and the assumption from which it proceeds have had in shaping the American just war doctrine. And while it would surely be unwarranted to dismiss as negligible the influence of the position sketched out above, there is perhaps even less warrant to consider that influence decisive. The American doctrine is not primarily the result of political and moral speculation engendered by nuclear technology, though it is very much the consequence of identifying force with total force. The new technology did not create that identification, though to many it has appeared to verify it in a manner that no longer permits of any doubt.

If the American doctrine of the just war does not acknowledge the political and moral dilemmas to which its proscription of force may give rise, this reluctance to do so must be attributed primarily to the traditional American interpretation of conflict. It has already been noted that this interpretation insists not only that force should not be employed aggressively as an instrument of national policy but that it need not be so employed—that somehow a nation may insure its security through means other than force. The possibility is therefore precluded that at some point the choice may have to be made either to resort to force in order to preserve the other interests of policy, though perhaps thereby transgressing the bounds of the moral law governing the resort to force, or to conform to the inhibitions imposed by the moral law, though perhaps thereby sacrificing the other interests of policy.[29] Given the optimism that informs the

---

[28] Unless, of course, one insists upon identifying order—any order—with justice. But this identification, too, is not compelling.

[29] We speak of "other interests" because the condemnation of force as an instrument of national policy is itself an "interest" of policy. Obviously, it is not the only interest, however, and the dilemma imposed upon the states-

American interpretation of conflict, this dilemma should never arise, since a necessary coincidence is assumed to exist between the circumstances in which doctrine legitimizes the employment of force and the actual circumstances in which the security interests of nations may be so endangered that force appears to be the only effective response if those interests are to be preserved.

It is instructive to view the policy of containment in the light of this traditional interpretation of conflict. Containment had its origin in what was held to be a situation of general insecurity resulting from the failure to establish a stable international order on the basis of the political solidarity of the victorious Powers of World War II, principally the United States and the Soviet Union. Containment was presented as a response to the expansionist policies of the Soviet Union, and its justification was that it sought to create an international environment in which this nation, and other nations as well, could enjoy a reasonable measure of security and the prospect of working out their destinies in freedom. Yet the restraints placed upon the use of force by a doctrine which, from the start, formed a corollary of the policy of containment, afforded no rational explanation save by assuming what was otherwise denied—that is, an international order capable of providing for nations a minimum framework of security. However suitable these restraints might have been for the order of preponderant centralized power originally envisaged by the framers of the Charter of the United Nations, they could hardly fail to give rise to considerable difficulty when applied to the policy of containment and to the order presupposed by that policy. For the legal and moral restraints placed upon the use of force cannot of themselves constitute an effective political order. They are rather the expression of a certain scheme or method

man lies precisely in the necessity to choose at some point between this interest and the other interests of policy.

for the organization of power. Whether that scheme will give rise to an effective order cannot be determined simply by analyzing the nature of these normative restraints. It must be determined instead by examining the character of political reality and by comparing this reality with the nature of the restraints which are intended to regulate it.

Whatever the ideological necessities under which American policy may have to operate, the order of containment was never the order of the Charter. It may of course be asserted that the purposes of containment and hence the ends for which American power has been employed have been coincidental with the purposes of the Charter. Nevertheless, the relevant point is that a policy of containment has sought to create and maintain a semblance of order and security, not by the methods of the Charter, but by the traditional method of countering a hostile and expansionist Power with power.

It is quite true that the logic governing a policy of containment need not be construed as implying that force must be threatened or employed on every occasion in which the object is to prevent an unfavorable change in the distribution of power. But is it possible to interpret such a policy as implying that the threat or use of force need not *ultimately* be governed by the necessity of preventing a serious deterioration in the balance of power? If not, then the "necessities" implicit in the policy of containment were never really compatible with the restrictions on the use of force that were contained, at least according to our interpretation, in the Charter of the United Nations. And since these restrictions of the Charter have always been held to reflect the requirements of the moral law, the political necessities of containment have never been easily reconciled with the requirements of the American doctrine of the just war.

Nor could a meaningful reconciliation be made between the necessities of containment and the requirements imposed by the American just war doctrine simply by the optimistic assumption of a necessary coincidence. Whether or not there is such a coincidence cannot be resolved by the optimistic assumption that a meaningful parallel exists between domestic and international society with respect to the relationship of force to order and security; that coincidence can be borne out only by experience. And if experience has taught any lesson, it is that this assumption is a hazardous one even when applied to periods during which the international society enjoys both a marked stability and a substantial consensus on the principles of international order. It may become almost ludicrous, however, when applied to a period in which the dominant members of the international society no longer agree even on the general principles of order, let alone on the concrete expression to be given these principles. It is the mark of such a period that the security problem is transformed from a concern that may nevertheless be "lived with" into an obsession that must somehow be "resolved." States may continue to express their grievances in traditional ways, and particularly their claims to possess a reasonable measure of security. But once conflict centers over the very principles on which international order is to be based, it is no longer simply by the satisfaction of any specific claim that the insecurity experienced by the antagonists can be alleviated. It is the terrible feature of such conflicts that what the contestants increasingly come to find incompatible with their security is not so much the specific claims advanced by the adversary but the latter's very existence.[30]

[30] While it is painfully apparent that the capacity for dealing sudden and complete destruction which the new technology has conferred must in any event very seriously aggravate the security problem, it is nevertheless an error to look upon this problem simply as a reflection of the existing technology for waging war. Sec. John Herz, *International Politics in the Atomic Age* (1959) . The desire to "resolve" the security problem, if necessary through the annihilation of the adversary, is not novel. Other periods have known

For a limited period, however, the dilemma thereby created for American policy remained little more than a distasteful prospect, due to what must now appear as quite transient and fortuitous circumstances. Yet in view of the optimism upon which the policy of containment was based, it was not surprising that these circumstances were interpreted as enduring realities, serving only as further confirmation for the deeply rooted belief that the necessities of policy and the requirements of the moral law were entirely compatible. The preferred methods of containment were of course economic and political, and at the time containment was adopted, it seemed only natural to assume that America's economic preponderance when coupled with the attractive power of American ideals of freedom and justice would prove sufficient to deal with any challenges to containment short of the overt employment of armed force.

The policy of containment did not thereby deliberately subordinate all other interests to the interest in peace. Nor did it reflect the conviction that, if necessary, peace must be placed above justice. Critics might point out that this policy would have the effect of making peace in the literal sense the supreme goal of policy. Though not without merit, this criticism nevertheless seemed to miss the point. If containment appeared to place an interest in peace above other interests, the explanation must be found in the assumption that peace formed the necessary and sufficient condition for the realization of these other interests. If containment appeared to place "peace before justice," the explanation must be found in the assumption that peace would eventually

this desire; and despite the extraordinary difficulties encountered in the past in bringing about its effective realization, men have not been deterred from this objective simply because of the primitive character of the means placed at their disposal. However profound the impact of the new technology, the ease with which annihilation can be carried out today is not the heart of the security problem. Instead, it is the willingness to contemplate using the new technology for this purpose.

bring justice. Containment reflected the belief that the changes which would occur if force were not resorted to would be of a certain character, that these changes would conform to our interests as a nation and prove compatible with our vision of a just international order. The essential prerequisite for the realization of our aspirations was that armed aggression be prevented. If our adversaries could be inhibited from employing force, if international society could once achieve at least this minimum form of security, our natural advantages would presumably insure eventual victory over the forces of darkness.[31]

[31] Indeed, it is only in retrospect that the marked optimism that initially informed the policy of containment can be fully appreciated. Observers, both within and outside government, could and did differ on the precise consequences of what were conceived to be our natural and enduring advantages. To a George Kennan they were interpreted to mean that the expression of containment should remain primarily political and economic, and even spiritual. In this view, the Marshall Plan stands out as the ideal measure of containment. This is not to say, however, that the instrument of force was excluded as a possible, and in certain circumstances a clearly necessary, measure. In his well-known "X" article, Kennan himself had spoken of the necessity of containing Soviet expansion "by the adroit and vigilant application of counterforce at a series of constantly shifting geographical and political points," and the entire force of his argument seemed to point to the conclusion that the threat or use of force must be the ultimate method of containment and that the choice of methods must be governed by the circumstances in which the purposes of containment had to be sought. Whatever the results that a logical interpretation of Kennan's argument would seem to imply, it is now apparent that these were not the results Kennan intended. Joseph G. Whelan is no doubt right when he points out that: "Containment in the sense of balancing Soviet power with alliances, guns and soldiers has never been a vital part of Kennan's thought. . . . That force plays a continuous and dynamic role in international politics does not seem to enter into his ideas at all." "George Kennan and His Influence on American Foreign Policy," *Virginia Quarterly Review*, xxx (Spring, 1954), 219-20. Yet the significant point for the discussion here is the consensus that existed, despite all other differences, on the central point that America's natural advantages—i.e., our economic preponderance and the strength of our ideals—would prove sufficient for dealing with the variety of situations in which containment was challenged by methods falling short of overt armed aggression.

On the other hand, the American doctrine of the just war was admirably suited to any challenges made to containment which took the form of overt armed aggression. Nor could the standards of the Charter be considered as constituting an obstacle in the event the need arose to use force in order to resist armed attack. Although generally forbidding the use of force by member states, the Charter clearly permitted the resort to force as a measure of individual or collective defense against an armed attack. In implementing the policy of containment by the organization of a military coalition to resist further Communist expansion, the conclusion of collective defense arrangements was represented as no more than the exercise of a right granted by the Charter. The experience of Korea overshadows all other events of this earlier period; although Korea provided the sole example of overt armed aggression by a Communist Power, it would be difficult to exaggerate its impact on the development of American policy generally, and particularly on the further expansion of the American alliance system.[32]

Even so, it was always recognized that "borderline" situations must be expected to arise and that these marginal

---

[32] To Secretary Dulles the "profound lesson" of Korea was the striking confirmation it provided for the belief that war results through the miscalculation of the aggressor. In an address devoted to Korean problems and delivered in St. Louis on September 2, 1953, Mr. Dulles developed a theme he was to repeat on a number of occasions during his tenure as Secretary of State. "Peace requires anticipating what it is that tempts an aggressor and letting him know in advance that, if he does not exercise self-control, he may face a hard fight, perhaps a losing fight. The Korean war—the third such war in our generation—should finally have taught us that, if we can foresee aggression which will cause us to fight, we should let this be known, so that the potential aggressor will take this into calculation." (*Bulletin*, xxix, 339.) Thus the twin pillars of peace and security must consist in a "political warning system"—i.e., collective defense arrangements predicated for their operation upon the contingency of armed attack or armed aggression—and "selective retaliatory power." When joined together, these two elements would inhibit if not altogether prevent the danger that war would result through the miscalculation of aggressors.

situations might well prove to be the true test of policy. American policy has never been so blinded by the imperatives of the moral law governing the employment of force as to neglect altogether the ordinary precautions of statecraft. If doctrine required that the just war be one waged only in self or collective defense against an armed attack, the practical task for policy became one of interpreting the concept of armed attack so as to fit the requirements of containment. That task was facilitated from the start by the view that what constitutes an armed attack is not at all self-evident and that, in any event, care must be exercised so as not to impute too great a rigidity to this standard. "When you come to real situations," Secretary Acheson declared at the time of the ratification of the North Atlantic Treaty, "you ought to be able to have some latitude in deciding them."[33] Neither under the Charter nor under the North Atlantic Pact was there any specific definition of what constitutes an armed attack, and this, Mr. Acheson insisted, was as it should be. Secretary Dulles may have professed greater confidence than did his predecessor in the objective quality of the requirements imposed by the moral law, but he never succeeded in improving on nor did he ever substantially deviate from Mr. Acheson's position.[34]

---

[33] Press Conference, March 18, 1949 (*The New York Times,* March 19, 1949). In the Senate hearings on the North Atlantic Treaty, Senator Fulbright asked: "Would an internal revolution, perhaps aided and abetted by an outside state, in which armed force was being used in an attempt to drive the recognized government from power be deemed an 'armed attack' within the meaning of article 5 [of the treaty]?" Secretary Acheson replied that he thought "it would be an armed attack." Senate Committee on Foreign Relations Hearing, *North Atlantic Treaty* (81st Cong., 1st Sess.), Part I, p. 59.

[34] A perfect illustration of Secretary Dulles' perennial endeavor to reconcile purity of doctrine and effectiveness of policy may be found in his Senate Testimony on the so-called Eisenhower Doctrine for the Middle East. Senate Committee on Foreign Relations Hearings, *The President's Proposal on the Middle East* (85th Cong., 1st Sess.), Part I. In responding to the

Thus the American just war doctrine has not been interpreted as precluding application of the concept of armed
attack to situations in which internal disorder or revolution
are supported in varying degree by an outside Power. Both
the Truman and the Eisenhower administrations have been
committed to the position that at least certain forms of
"indirect aggression" might be assimilated to the concept
of armed attack, thereby justifying the resort to force as a
measure of self or collective defense, though the nature of
the circumstances in which indirect aggression may be held
to justify the use of force remains as obscure today as at
the outset of Soviet-American rivalry.

There are perhaps no readily discernible limits to the
disparate situations which may be interpreted as coming
within the scope of a just war doctrine. But there are limits
to the satisfaction that can be derived from this time-honored
method of insuring that the requirements of a just war doctrine will somehow always coincide with the necessities of
policy. What must at least be acknowledged as a theoretical

criticism that the Middle Eastern resolution was too restrictive, being limited
to cases of "overt armed aggression," Mr. Dulles declared: ". . . we are
saying that we are going to live up to our obligation in the Charter of
the United Nations and in all . . . of our mutual security treaties, that
we only act militarily for defense in case an armed attack occurs . . . the
idea that the only way to deal with these problems [i.e., subversion] is by
military invasion of a country is, I think, a false and an obsolete idea . . .
we do not use force except as the other fellow uses it first. And if you
change that principle and say that it is permissible to use force except for
defense, then I think that you are setting the clock back in a way which
is very, very dangerous indeed" (pp. 27-29). Yet in reply to a question by
Senator Knowland as to what action the United States might take in the
hypothetical situation in which Iran would have a Communist-controlled
government and "invite the Soviet Union to send into Iran Soviet armored
divisions," Secretary Dulles responded that we might well consider this situation to constitute an armed attack, though we would not then be acting
under the terms of the Middle Eastern resolution. Mr. Dulles added: "Now
we may act for other reasons of our own interest, and that is not excluded
at all, I think, by this resolution, and I do not think it should be . . ."
(pp. 139-40).

possibility—that is, the divergence between the standards of a just war doctrine and the necessities of successful policy—is to all intents and purposes precluded as a practical possibility, given only the attribution of sufficient flexibility to the standards governing the resort to force and the insistence that the interpretation of these standards must be left to the interested parties. In this manner, modern just war doctrines share the fate of their predecessors in becoming scarcely distinguishable from mere ideologies the purpose of which is to provide a spurious justification for almost any use of force.

It is only natural that we should comfort ourselves with the conviction that we have successfully withstood a temptation to which other nations have succumbed. Unfortunately, the sincerity of this conviction affords no justification for its uncritical acceptance. Nor is it sufficient to insist, in the words of Secretary Dulles, that the American people "can understand, and will support policies which can be explained and understood in moral terms," but that "policies merely based on carefully calculated expediency could never be explained and would never be understood." [35] However deep-rooted the American desire to "understand" policy as the mere reflection of principles whose universal validity is unquestioned, this desire is no guarantee that the understanding will be little more than an illusion.

This is not to suggest, however, that the devotion American statesmen profess toward what they constantly proclaim as inviolable principle is simply an empty ritual, interesting in terms of its excesses but devoid of any consequence for policy. If the American just war doctrine has served an ideological function, this ought not to obscure recognition that it has also transcended the purely ideological. The past decade and a half furnishes a number of instances in which

[35] Address to American Legion, Miami, Fla., October 10, 1955 (*Bulletin*, XXXIII, 640).

the attempt to reconcile the political requirements for effectively containing communist power with what have been
deemed inviolable moral imperatives respecting the use of
force has clearly formed a significant issue. The endeavor to
expand the limits of the concept of armed attack may demonstrate the limits of "pure" moral conviction, particularly
when divorced from political realities, but that endeavor
has also demonstrated the persistence of moral conviction.
For the indecision and uncertainty that have marked the
role of force in contemporary American policy must be
attributed in substantial measure to a doctrine which has
seemingly compelled us either to purchase political success
at the price of a uneasy conscience or to retain a good conscience at the risk of courting political failure.

It is particularly in those marginal situations in which
the application of professed international standards is clearly
not self-evident that the insistence by interested parties on
a final right of interpretation is bound to create a suspicion
not easily dissipated and to lend substance to the charge
that these standards have been subverted. Given the intense
and undoubtedly the sincere desire of this nation to justify
its behavior, both to itself and to the world at large, this
charge could but give rise to unease. In the early years
of containment the conviction that moral uncertainty would
be resolved by entrusting to the United Nations General
Assembly the task of providing an "objective" interpretation
of the Charter's standards appeared as an almost perfect
solution to the anxiety thus created, an almost perfect solution because it would lessen anxiety without requiring the
essential modification of policy. To make the General Assembly the true interpreter of the Charter's norms, to elevate
that body from a mere global "town meeting" to the embodi-
ment of the world's conscience and guardian of the moral
law surely corresponded more to traditional American senti-
ments and aspirations than did the original hierarchical order

of power envisaged by the framers of the Charter. In view of the commanding position enjoyed by this nation in the General Assembly during this period, the existing identity of interests between the United States and at least two-thirds of the members of the Assembly seemed as good an insurance as could be expected that a similar identity would prevail between the dicta of the world's conscience and the necessities of American policy.

Thus the doubt that might otherwise arise over whether the use of force in a given instance conformed to the Charter and to the moral law would be removed by the General Assembly. The "Uniting For Peace" resolution, inspired by the United States and passed by the Assembly in November, 1950, provided the formal mechanism for distinguishing between the legitimate and illegitimate employment of force. In urging the acceptance of that resolution, John Foster Dulles, then a member of the American delegation to the United Nations, declared that the United States believed that the Assembly would reflect "better than any other body, the supremacy of 'law,' which in essence is the consensus of world opinion as to what is right." [36]

The period that witnessed these developments has come to an end, however, and the circumstances that made these developments possible and related them in a meaningful way to American policy have substantially changed. If it is claiming too much to assert that the optimism attending this earlier period of containment has disappeared, it is reasonably clear that it lives on only in a very attenuated form. We are no longer so certain, in the words of Secretary Acheson, that "time is on our side" and that all we need do is prevent the resort to overt aggression while exploiting our natural advantages. We may still believe, as Secretary Dulles insistently maintained, that "free governments in the long run

[36] Statement to Political Committee of the General Assembly, October 9, 1959 (*Bulletin*, xxiii[2], 658).

are going to prevail and despotic governments in the long run are going to go under," but the long run now appears appreciably longer than in the early period of containment. In the meantime, policy must address itself to the short run. To be sure, the containment of Communist power remains the central feature of American policy. Yet the meaning imputed to containment has undergone significant change. The early assumption of an enduring preponderance of power has slowly and almost imperceptibly given way to the aspiration to maintain a balance of power. Whereas this early assumption of a preponderance of power formed the basis for conceiving of a policy of containment as constituting merely the necessary prelude to the eventual collapse or at least the substantial modification of Soviet power, the aspiration to maintain a balance reflects an interpretation of containment more nearly in accord with the literal meaning of that term. The confident assertion of Mr. Acheson may readily have appeared an indisputable statement of fact in the early 1950's. The equally confident assertions of Mr. Dulles several years later no longer conveyed the same assurance and appeared to border on the oracular.

If, in these altered circumstances, an ever-greater emphasis is placed on methods of containment which stop short of the employment of force, the reason for this emphasis is no longer so much the optimism initially inspiring containment as it is fear of the consequences that might follow from any resort to force. Nevertheless, the dilemma of reconciling the requirements of a just war doctrine with the requirements of effective policy must still be distinguished from the problem resulting from a growing disproportion between the interests to be protected by resorting to force and the risks incurred in employing force. Both considerations point up the difficulty of the task of establishing a rational relationship between force and policy.

However, the American doctrine of the just war does not stem primarily from the conviction that the hazards presently incurred by any resort to force have become increasingly disproportionate to the worth of most of the other interests of policy, whatever additional support this conviction may provide. Unless it is assumed that these hazards have destroyed completely the possibility of effecting a rational relationship between force and policy, the possibility must remain of a serious divergence between the necessities of policy and the imperatives of a just war doctrine. Indeed, it is clear that this divergence will become increasingly probable precisely because the risks involved in the overt resort to armed aggression place a correspondingly increased premium upon the variety of measures loosely labelled as "indirect aggression." The dilemma of having to choose between the action that may be required of successful policy and the inhibitions imposed by the moral law is not lessened in a world where any resort to force may lead to unlimited nuclear war; if anything, the dilemma may be markedly accentuated.

In the present context, then, an unwillingness to resolve this dilemma either by sacrificing policy to doctrine, or by so interpreting unilaterally the standards of a just war doctrine as to insure the coincidence of policy and doctrine, leaves only the alternative of obtaining the mandate of the General Assembly before employing force in circumstances which do not clearly constitute armed aggression. But the conditions that once produced an identity of interests between the United States and a sufficient majority of the member states of the Assembly to make this an attractive alternative have progressively given way to a situation in which the United States has lost a substantial measure of the initiative and the commanding position it formerly enjoyed. The present composition and temper of the Assembly are such that the only type of resolution offering a sound prospect of securing the required support is one condemning the initial resort to armed force, without regard either for the other circumstances that may attend such resort to force or for the nature of the interests to be protected by openly employing force. Given the present disparity of interests in the General Assembly, it is peace in the pure and literal sense of the term that constitutes the one interest capable of obtaining an Assembly mandate. That interest has perhaps found its clearest expression to date in the Assembly's "impartial" condemnation of armed intervention, whether by the Soviet Union in Hungary or by Israel, Great Britain, and France in Egypt.

These considerations suggest that in terms of the effective implementation of American policy, the usefulness of the Assembly can no longer be relied upon. Of this, the marked refusal of the Assembly to sanction the American action in sending military forces into Lebanon in the summer of 1958, though at the formal request of the Lebanese government, was a clear forewarning. Still more critical and far more ambiguous contingencies can be envisaged in which the Assembly could well come to represent a positive obstacle to American policy. It is not difficult to conceive of a situation in which Berlin could become the American Suez, at least as far as the General Assembly is concerned. For it has long been apparent that the preservation of West Berlin's status depends upon our willingness, in the last resort, to take the initiative in resorting to armed force. Our refusal to acknowledge this is readily understandable, but it does not change the nature of the situation. The impeding of the Western Powers' right of access to Berlin would constitute the violation of a legal right. Yet the violation of a legal right is not to be confused with armed aggression—or, for that matter, even with "indirect aggression." In sending an armored force into East Germany in order to remove any impediments to our right of access to Berlin, we would commit the first act of violence. To claim that we would never, as President Eisenhower has solemnly declared, "fire the first shot," and therefore would never be open to the charge of having committed armed aggression, is almost to introduce a note of levity into this situation. Why not carry this reasoning further, and assume that the Soviet or East German forces meet an armored force with an armored force but also refrain from firing the first shot. Do both sides then silently push each other around, each waiting for the other to fire the first shot and thereby to commit "armed aggression"? Berlin also provides a good example of circumstances that may require both a liberal and a literal interpretation of the international standards alleged to govern the use of force. It may well prove useful to assimilate the act of impeding our access to Berlin to that of an armed attack or an armed aggression. At the same time, the act of sending an armored force into East Germany to remove any impediment may be characterized as a legitimate measure of self-defense, not only for the professed reason that this measure would be taken in response to armed aggression but for the further reason that we would refrain from "firing the first shot." [37]

Whether in these circumstances the alternative of entrusting the interpretation of the moral law to the Assembly will continue to prove acceptable to this nation cannot be answered with any real degree of assurance. It is difficult to believe, however, that if a clear and serious divergence arose between the Assembly's interpretation of the requirements

[37] The latter justification, however absurd, has frequently been invoked in support of our intervention in the Chinese civil war following the outbreak of the Korean conflict. In this "impartial neutralizing action" not a shot was fired. Yet in 1955 Secretary Dulles indicated that we might be forced to fire the first shot, though of course only in self-defense, if in our judgment Chinese Communist "actions, preparations and concentrations in the Formosa area constituted in fact the first phase of an attack directed against Taiwan. . . ." Statement to Press, Taipei, Formosa, March 3, 1955, (*Bulletin* xxxii, 421).

of the moral law and our interpretation of the necessities imposed upon American policy, the latter would be sacrificed. Nevertheless, any action taken in opposition to an Assembly judgment would not only represent a severe political defeat but, what is more significant for this discussion, it would almost certainly give rise to a genuine "crisis of conscience." Cynical observers may contend that the American obsession with the United Nations is a rare illustration in statecraft of how sincerity can become indistinguishable from hypocrisy. In fact, the American attitude toward the United Nations—and, since the cold war began, toward its principal organ, the General Assembly—is better characterized as an example of how a doctrine that is based upon a sufficient degree of self-deception has no need to be devious.

Our conviction that the collective judgment of the Assembly may best reflect the moral law is no less sincere than our belief that the Assembly will only realize its true role when its judgments do not contradict American desires and interests. No one perhaps reflected this thoroughly ambivalent attitude toward the Assembly better than John Foster Dulles. In urging the Assembly's acceptance of the "Uniting For Peace" resolution in 1950, Mr. Dulles may have asserted the conviction that the Assembly would reflect "better than any other body, the supremacy of 'law' which in essence is the consensus of world opinion as to what is right." At the same time, he cautioned that if for some reason the Assembly did not realize its potentiality, it would "automatically fail for, in these matters, moral judgments are our only reliable dependency." [38] Eight years later, in his last public address, Secretary Dulles returned to the same theme in declaring that although the General Assembly "can be and is powerful when it reflects a genuine moral judgment," its claim to

[38] See note 36 above.

represent humanity's aspirations to peace through law and justice would be impaired, if not altogether destroyed, were it to endorse a "permanent double standard" or to develop into a "system of bloc voting in terms of geographical areas or in terms of the 'haves' as against the 'have nots.'"[39] The first of Mr. Dulles' strictures was intended as a reproval of the Assembly's alleged recent tolerance of the activities of the Soviet bloc and an indication that more condemnation of and effective action against these activities were expected. The warning against developing into a system of bloc voting was an obvious allusion to the marked tendency in recent years to turn the Assembly from a forum in which the Soviet bloc would be arraigned and judged by the world's moral conscience into a forum in which colonial powers would be arraigned and judged by anticolonial powers.

The emphasis in 1958 may have been quite different from the emphasis in 1950, but there is no apparent inconsistency between these views. For the willingness with which this nation has championed the General Assembly as the most appropriate instrument for registering the moral consensus of humanity and the sincerity with which we have sought to conform in our actions to the judgments of the Assembly have always been attended by the insistence that the Assembly's judgments must be the "right" judgments. Thus in undertaking to subordinate our judgment to the collective judgment of the Assembly in cases of "indirect aggression,"

[39] Address to New York State Bar Assn., January 31, 1959 (*Bulletin*, XL, 258-59). There is a special irony in our complaint that of late the General Assembly has seemed to support a "double standard." In the disparity that marked the position and privileges of the permanent members of the Security Council and the other members of the United Nations, it was the "old" or original Charter that clearly supported a double standard. The "new" Charter in which the General Assembly has supplanted the Security Council as the primary organ of the United Nations has one standard; that is the significance of the "new" Charter and, at the same time, its principal difficulty. If our complaint has any meaning, then, it is that the one standard is effective for some states and ineffective for other states.

our stated expectation has been that the Assembly's judgments will "objectively" reflect the requirements of justice. In the Lebanese action, to take a recent example, the Eisenhower administration followed the pattern marked out by its predecessor in undertaking to withdraw emergency assistance to Lebanon whenever the United Nations General Assembly found such assistance to be no longer necessary. The issue of indirect aggression, Secretary Dulles conceded some weeks following the July 1958 landing of American troops in Lebanon, was a very delicate one. "On the one hand, it is clear, beyond a possibility of a doubt, that nations are free to seek, and to get, help as against a genuine external threat. On the other hand, we must be careful not to encourage or condone armed intervention, which of itself may subvert the will of a foreign people." For these reasons, Mr. Dulles concluded, the United States believed "that the task of dealing with indirect aggression should so far as possible be assumed by the United Nations itself. That will eliminate the hazard that individual nations might use armed intervention under circumstances that were self-serving rather than serving the principles of the Charter." [40] At the same time, the Secretary warned that the General Assembly could assume this function only if it were able to act effectively in cases of indirect aggression and if its actions conformed to the objective requirements of justice. Given this attitude, only the obtuse will persist in asking whether what we want is objectivity from the Assembly in interpreting the moral law or support for American policy. The answer cannot be in doubt: we want, and expect, both.

Thus our championing of the General Assembly has been a nice mixture of our obsession for moral certainty and of our desire to employ that body as a political instrument in support of American policy. Should the Assembly prove

---

[40] Address to VFW, New York, August 18, 1958 (*Bulletin,* xxxix, 373-76).

unwilling to lend itself to the support of American policy in the future, the occasion could conceivably arise in which we would consciously choose to place ourselves in open conflict with what we have heretofore regarded as the "collective judgment of the world community." In a sense, the justification for making such a choice has been implicit from the start in the very ambivalence with which we have viewed the Assembly. This nation has not been deterred in the past from employing force, though with no other apparent justification than the bare assertion that our security interests required such action.[41] There is no compelling reason for believing that we would forego the use of force in the future in order to conform to a positive injunction of the Assembly. But it is another matter to assert that the latter situation would not give rise to considerable unease, particularly if, as must be expected, the circumstances in which the use of force is contemplated are ambiguous and difficult to fit into the mold of the American doctrine of the just war. More important still is the consideration that the task of providing a satisfactory moral justification for the employment of force would not only remain but would become, in all probability, considerably more difficult to resolve. For the Assembly has been an asset as well as a liability. Whatever

[41] In placing American naval forces between Formosa and the Chinese mainland in June, 1950, President Truman characterized the measure as a matter of "elementary security," designed to prevent the extension of the conflict then going on in Korea. Message to Congress, July 19, 1950 (*Bulletin*, xxiii[1], 166). Whatever the merit of the justification given for intervening in a conflict that we had previously insisted upon regarding as a purely internal affair, neither the Security Council nor the General Assembly sanctioned the measure. It is noteworthy that although Korea provided *the* model example of the reconciliation of doctrine and policy, one of the principal consequences of our response to the Korean attack could be so reconciled only with considerable difficulty. It is not apparent that the conflict in Korea conferred on this nation any rights with respect to the Chinese conflict that had not been possessed before the outbreak of the Korean hostilities.

the inhibitions it has placed, and may yet place, upon the effective implementation of American policy, it has provided a basis for justifying certain actions not only to the world but to ourselves as well.

IV

If war can be undertaken only in defense against armed aggression, the purposes sought in waging such a war or in preparing against the possibility of such a war must also be defensive in character. This, as least, is the assumption upon which the American doctrine of the just war rests, and that assumption is seldom questioned. How, indeed, can the purposes of war be considered as anything other than defensive if force is employed only in response to armed aggression? What other objectives can peace-loving nations have, once they are attacked, save to defend themselves and to insure, as far as it lies within their power, that the aggressor will never again have the opportunity or the will to pursue his evil designs? And how can the intrinsic justice of these purposes—defense and peace—be denied or their intent be doubted?

The self-evident character of the purposes we seek in resorting to war or in preparing against aggression is proverbial. Thus each of the military alignments into which we have entered is—as Senator Vandenberg once described the North Atlantic Treaty—a "fraternity of peace" whose obvious purpose is to preserve peace by deterring aggression.[42] "We do not arm for purposes of conquest," Secretary

[42] It is perhaps relevant to recall that the Senate hearings on the North Atlantic Treaty were dominated by the care with which the treaty was distinguished from the traditional military alliance. Senator Vandenberg declared that in his judgment "the traditional interpretation of the phrase 'military alliance' carries within it an offensive rather than an essentially defensive overriding objective, and that it is a partnership for power rather

Acheson declared on the eve of American rearmament in 1950, "our strength is a shield. . . ."[43] "Man has often used military force to *restore* peace," the American military commander of NATO recently observed, "but NATO is the finest example of its use to *preserve* peace."[44] And in a reply to a letter of Bertrand Russell, Secretary Dulles placed the matter in its broadest perspective by appealing both to the moral law and to history. "The creed of the United States is based on the tenets of moral law. That creed, as well as the universal conviction of the United States, rejects war except in self-defense. . . . I do not think that it is possible to find in the history of the United States any occasion when an effort has been made to spread its creed by force of arms."[45]

than a partnership for peace." Senate Committee on Foreign Relations Hearings, *North Atlantic Treaty* (81st Cong., 1st Sess.), Part I, p. 143. Senator Connally characterized the treaty as "an alliance for peace . . . and against war itself" (p. 150). A State Department memorandum on the differences between the North Atlantic Treaty and traditional military alliances stated: "All traditional military alliances, in the accepted sense of the word, were designed to advance the respective nationalistic interests of the parties, and provided for joint military action if one of the parties in pursuit of such objectives became involved in war" (p. 334). But NATO, the memorandum went on to insist, was a pure application of collective security: "It is directed against no one: it is directed solely against aggression. It seeks not to influence any shifting 'balance of power' but to strengthen the 'balance of principle'" (p. 337). Similar characterizations have been made of later military alignments into which the United States has entered.

[43] Address at Harvard University, Cambridge, Mass., June 22, 1950 (*Bulletin*, XXIII, 18).

[44] General Lauris Norstad. Address to the American Council on NATO, New York, January 29, 1957 (*Bulletin*, XXXVI, 251). In this speech General Norstad went on to observe that: "Should it ever be necessary for us to defend ourselves, this allied command can and will play its full part in destroying the aggressor" (p. 253). Here, as elsewhere, the equation of defense both with deterring an aggressor and with destroying the aggressor, should deterrence fail, is simply taken as self-evident.

[45] Letter to Kingsley Martin in reply to letter of Bertrand Russell, February 6, 1958 (*Bulletin*, XXXVIII, 290). And in a statement following this novel interpretation of certain chapters of American history, Mr. Dulles,

Potential aggressors cannot but be aware of our true purposes. Hence, they can have no legitimate cause to fear either our security arrangements or the defensive and peaceful purposes these arrangements are designed to fulfill. "A 'showdown,' in the brutal and realistic sense of resort to a military decision is not a possible policy for a democracy. The Kremlin knows that."[46] These reassuring words of Dean Acheson have been echoed countless times and with obvious sincerity by American political and military leaders. If the Soviets have not always appeared fully appreciative of our purposes and intention, if as General Gruenther once observed, "they do not understand that our alliance [NATO] is clearly a defensive one and that our objective is the preservation of peace, it [can] only be a distorted philosophy which blinds them."[47] Occasionally the pathological outlook of the aggressor is subjected to more detached consideration. "To us their [Soviet's] fears seem mere pretense," Secretary Dulles once reflected, "but perhaps they do have fear, because they do not understand that if force is in the hands of those who are governed by moral law, it will not be used as a means of aggression or to violate the principles of the moral law."[48]

quite characteristically, added: "While of course nuclear war is the form of war most to be dreaded . . . the essential is to avoid war of any kind, nuclear or nonnuclear, and to renounce all use of force as a means of subjecting human beings to a rule to which they do not freely consent."

[46] Remarks to Advertising Council, White House, February 16, 1950 (*Bulletin*, xxii[1], 427) .

[47] Address at Alfred E. Smith Memorial Foundation Dinner, October 8, 1953 (*Bulletin*, xxix, 635) .

[48] Address to National War College, June 16, 1953 (*Bulletin*, xxviii, 897) . The conviction that potential aggressors can have no legitimate reason to fear any of the security measures we may take was strikingly illustrated by the widely publicized U-2 incident. At his first press conference on May 11, 1960, following the Soviet announcement of the capture of an American aircraft and pilot engaged in aerial reconnaisance over the Soviet Union, President Eisenhower responded to Soviet charges of provocation by heatedly declaring that: ". . . the United States and none of its Allies that I know of

What the moral law permits in order to deter aggression and to preserve peace, it must equally permit in order to resist aggression and to restore peace. In either case, the purposes sought are the same—defense and peace—and the only questions that remain concern the most effective means for realizing these objectives. The problems of deterring or resisting aggression are thereby transformed into "technical" questions governed by political, military, and of course, economic considerations. Is massive atomic and thermonuclear retaliation the kind of power "which could most usefully be invoked under all circumstances"? "How should collective defense be organized by the free world for maximum protection at minimum cost?" These are the technical questions to be resolved by what Secretary Dulles termed the "science of peace," and they are the questions to which Mr. Dulles addressed himself in proclaiming the "new" strategy for deterring aggression.[49]

has engaged in nothing that would be considered honestly as provocative. We are looking to our own security and our defense and we have no idea of promoting any kind of conflict or war. This is just, it's absolutely ridiculous and they know it is." Transcript in *New York Times*, May 12, 1960, p. 14. In view of the Soviet Union's "fetish of secrecy and concealment" the President insisted that these "overflights" represented no more than reasonable security measures taken against the possibility of massive surprise attack. And since the information gained from the U-2 flights would "obviously" be used only for strictly defensive purposes, the Soviet reaction was interpreted as one further example of the aggressor's inability to appreciate our peaceful intentions. The suggestion that the adversary might seriously fear that the intelligence gained from these overflights would enhance the feasibility of a preventive war—or a "pre-emptive attack"—was therefore indignantly dismissed.

[49] See John Foster Dulles, "Policy for Security and Peace," *Foreign Affairs*, xxxii (April, 1954), 353 ff. For one so profoundly committed to the belief that the use of power must always be closely disciplined by the requirements of the moral law, the very manner in which Secretary Dulles phrased these questions must prove to be of abiding interest. It is difficult not to believe, however, that the tenor of Mr. Dulles' discussion of the "technical" problems of deterring aggression would have shocked the moral sensibilities of an earlier, though an allegedly less moral, age. Not so the present age, with

Whatever political-military difficulties our policy of deterrence and of resistance to aggression may encounter and indeed has encountered, the moral basis and justification for this policy has remained substantially unchanged. For both the supporters and the critics of this policy, the nature of our purposes is regarded as self-evident, and their intrinsic moral worth is judged as being beyond dispute. In the continuing debate over military policy and particularly over the strategy of nuclear deterrence, the moral issues have therefore been regarded as rather irrelevant, not because they are looked upon as unimportant in themselves but because they are considered as settled and unchanging. Is a policy of nuclear deterrence always and everywhere credible to the potential aggressor? Are we prepared to invoke nuclear retaliation in certain areas and under ambiguous circumstances? Where and under what circumstances are we to confront a potential aggressor with the "sure prospect of his own annihilation" should he ever resort to an armed attack, and when is it expedient only to promise a would-be aggressor that he would suffer far more from the resort to force than he could possibly gain by taking this step? These are the questions the debate over the policy of nuclear deterrence has raised and continues to raise. But the quite different questions that concern the moral justification for this policy are seldom if ever raised. Indeed, even to raise such questions would be looked upon as an impropriety, since that would be interpreted as reflecting doubt upon the worthiness of our purposes. It is one thing to contend that there are political and military risks incurred by a commitment to deter potential aggressors with threats of destruc-

its certitude that it fulfills the requirements of the moral law. "Of all the illusions a people can cherish," John Bassett Moore warned in the aftermath of World War I, "the most extravagant and illogical is the supposition that, along with the progressive degradation of its standards of conduct, there is to go a progressive increase in respect for law and morality." *International Law and Some Current Illusions* (1924) , p. 24.

tion or severe punishment; it is quite another matter to suggest that there are also moral risks incurred by a policy of deterrence, and that these risks stem not only from the means employed or threatened by a policy of deterrence but even more from the purposes which may inform such a policy.

It is significant that even on those very rare occasions when the moral justification for American military strategy has been criticized, the criticism has been directed to the means or methods of warfare implicit, according to the critics, in this strategy and not to the purposes allegedly served by this strategy. In the 1949 hearings on the B-36 bomber program and the unification of the armed services, Navy spokesmen made much of the "immorality" of a method of warfare which, in their judgment, necessarily involved the indiscriminate bombing of cities.[50] Admiral Radford, who was to become in the 1950's one of the leading apostles of the pure theory of deterring aggressors through a reliance upon the threat of massive nuclear retaliation, declared that: "One member of the defense team in one branch of the government asserts that the best guaranty for America's security lies first in preventing war by the threat of atomic annihilation, and second in prosecuting such a war of annihilation if we have to fight."[51] This theory of a cheap and easy victory through an "atomic blitz," Admiral Radford went on to insist, was not only politically and militarily unsound but "morally reprehensible." "I don't believe in mass killing of non-combatants. . . . I am against indiscriminate bombing of cities," he stated, condemning at the same time the measures taken against enemy noncombatants during World War II by American and British air forces.[52] Never-

[50] See House Committee on Armed Services Hearings, *The National Defense Program—Unification and Strategy* (81st Cong., 1st Sess.).

[51] *Ibid.,* p. 50.

[52] *Ibid.,* pp. 56, 75. In responding to the case the Navy had made for the "moral wrong of mass bombing," General Omar Bradley declared that as

theless, Admiral Radford—and other Navy spokesmen as well—entertained no doubt about the nature of our purposes in any future war or the moral justification of those purposes. The Navy was as one with the other services in assuming that if war is forced upon us we must "win it," and win it completely, and that this objective was implicit in our purposes of defense and peace.[53] Later disputes over military strategy, and over the weapons systems to be employed in the implementation of strategy, have been marked by a similar consensus.

Thus the moral anxiety manifested about the circumstances in which states may legitimately resort to force has its counterpart in the moral complacency shown toward the objectives for which force may be employed against aggression. The intent of this doctrine is not to divorce the justice or injustice of war from the purposes sought in employing force. On the contrary, what distinguishes the American doctrine in this respect is the insistence with which it finds a necessary relationship between the circumstances in which force is initiated and the objectives for which force is em-

far as he was concerned "war itself is immoral," and concluded by noting that "if our attacks are only in retaliation for an attack made upon us, the American people may feel that strategic bombing is both militarily sound and morally justified" (p. 522).

[53] A decade later, however, the Navy had apparently forgotten its earlier objections to methods of warfare which might imply a commitment to the annihilation of an enemy's civilian population. On March 28, 1960 one of the *New York Times* military correspondents, Jack Raymond, reported that Navy pressure for a large fleet of Polaris submarines had met the objection—urged, ironically enough, by the Air Force—that the missiles fired by the Polaris were primarily city destroyers rather than counterforce weapons (i.e., weapons powerful and accurate enough to destroy tough military targets). Too great an emphasis on the weapons system represented by the Polaris would therefore run a substantial risk of committing the nation to a strategy of concentrating on the destruction of urban centers in the event of nuclear conflict rather than on military targets. The Navy, Raymond reports, "does not reject the need for some counter-force weapons. But it puts far less stress on them than the Air Force."

ployed. A preoccupation with the overt act of resorting to war leads to the assumption that the purposes of wars—and their justice or injustice—may be deduced from the circumstances in which war was initiated. In this manner the causes for resorting to war and the objectives sought in war converge and tend to become almost identical. The same principles of the moral law that sanction the resort to force must also sanction the purposes sought through force. The purposes of the aggressor, therefore, are by definition unjust, whereas the purposes of those fighting in self or collective defense against aggression must be just, again by definition.

Given the logic of this doctrine, a war fought for the end of "unconditional surrender" may be as much a defensive war, designed to restore peace, as a war which leaves the power and the boundaries of the aggressor substantially unchanged. Indeed, given the logic of this doctrine, a war fought to the end of unconditional surrender is much more faithful to the purposes of defense and peace. In exorcising the sources of aggression completely, one best fulfills these purposes. Thus the limited ends finally sought in the Korean conflict could not fail to appear as falling far short of the true purposes for which a defensive war should be waged. But even the Korean conflict provided an instructive example of the ease with which varying war aims could be encompassed within the purposes of defense and peace. "In reaching the great decisions on June 25 and 26," Walter Millis has written, "it had been assumed by all parties that the objective was simply to push the Communists back again behind the 38th Parallel boundary—in Truman's words, 'to restore peace there and to restore the border.'"[54] In an address to the nation on September 1, 1950, however, President Truman declared: "We believe the Koreans have a right to be free, independent, and united—as they want to be. Under the direction and guidance of the United Nations, we, with

[54] Walter Millis, *Arms and the State* (1958), p. 272.

others, will do our part to help them enjoy that right. The
United States has no other aim in Korea." [55] In the circum-
stances, this aim could hardly be achieved other than by
the invasion of North Korea and the complete defeat of the
North Korean forces. Accordingly, on October 1 the United
States and United Nations commander in Korea, General Mac-
Arthur, demanded the unconditional surrender of all enemy
forces in Korea, threatening them otherwise with "total defeat
and complete destruction." [56] Yet on April 30, 1951, Secretary
Acheson insisted that from the start this nation and the
United Nations as well, "never contemplated the use of
force to accomplish its political objective in Korea, which
is the establishment of a unified, independent, and democratic country." [57] On a later occasion, Secretary Acheson
reiterated this statement of American purposes in Korea and
defended the crossing of the 38th parallel the previous September by stating that the crossing was militarily necessary
in order to destroy or to capture the remaining North Korean
forces. If there had been no later intervention by the Chinese
Communists, Mr. Acheson added, "then there would probably have been a unification of Korea as a result of the
combat; but the combat was not for the purpose of doing
that. It was for the purpose of eliminating this aggression
by rounding up people who refused to surrender and who
refused to lay down their arms and refused to do anything
except keep on fighting." [58]

Despite the ingenuity of Mr. Acheson's explanation,
American war aims had obviously changed between September, 1950, and the spring of 1951. The significant point

[55] *Bulletin,* xxii[1], 409.

[56] Text of Surrender Terms to North Korean Forces, October 1, 1950
(*Bulletin,* xxiii[2], 586).

[57] *Bulletin,* xxiv[2], 769.

[58] Statement of June 26, 1951 to House Committee on Foreign Affairs
(House Committee on Foreign Affairs Hearings, *Mutual Security Program*
[82nd Cong., 1st Sess.], p. 25).

here, however, is the ease and undoubted sincerity with which it was contended throughout that American purposes were simply "to resist aggression and to restore peace." It is also worth observing that Korea furnishes an instructive example of our willingness to attain through force—once force is defensively undertaken against aggression—political ends that, prior to the resort to force, we have insisted must be obtained only by peaceful methods. To be sure, the "explanation" and consequently the justification for this apparent inconsistency is that the aggressor, by the very act of resorting to aggression, forfeits any right to claim that disputes—including territorial disputes—must be settled by negotiation rather than by superior force. Nevertheless, this justification cannot do away with the objection that the very means for achieving political objectives which may be condemned prior to the outbreak of hostilities become the means by which these objectives are realized once defensive war is undertaken.

At any rate, it is clear that given the logic of the American doctrine, a war which succeeds in radically changing the international order existing at the outbreak of war may have a purpose no different from that of a war which leaves that order substantially unchanged. So also, the attempt to deter a potential aggressor by threatening to visit him with the "sure prospect of his own annihilation," should he ever resort to armed aggression, is informed by the same defensive purpose as the attempt to deter potential aggressors by making clear that although any armed attack would be resisted, no more force than necessary would be used for repelling the attack and restoring the *status quo ante bellum*. What holds for the purpose of defense must hold equally for the purpose of peace; and what can be justified as a defensive measure, taken for the purpose of deterring or resisting aggression, can also be justified as a measure designed to maintain or to restore peace.

It is, of course, apparent that if the nature and purposes of a defensive war are to be given their traditional meaning, the conclusions to which the American doctrine leads must be regarded as no less fallacious than the reasoning by which these conclusions are reached. There is no necessary relationship, political or moral, between the circumstances that mark the initiation of war and the objectives sought in war. Neither in history nor in logic can it be demonstrated that a war initiated in circumstances of a defensive character must for this reason also be regarded as a war fought for defensive purposes. The military aggressor may, nevertheless, have defensive purposes in war and the state attacked may entertain purposes which, once in war, are clearly more than defensive. A war fought for the end of unconditional surrender can only with difficulty, if at all, be regarded as having a defensive purpose in the traditional sense, and this quite apart from the immediate circumstances in which the war began. For the obvious consequence of such a war must be to effect a radical change in the *status quo,* as regards both the power and vital interests of the victorious and defeated states and if the war involves major powers, the international order operative at the outbreak of war. And if the nature and purposes of a defensive war are to be understood in their traditional meaning, a similar judgment must be reached with respect to a policy that seeks to ward off armed aggression by threatening to destroy or to punish severely a potential aggressor should he once resort to armed force. Such a policy has a defensive nature and purpose only as long as the necessity to resort to armed force does not arise. But should armed aggression nevertheless occur, the active implementation of the threat can no longer be regarded as merely defensive.

To be sure, the limits traditionally imposed upon a war fought for defensive purposes cannot be defined with precision. But the fact that the limits of a defensive war cannot be defined with precision does not mean that they cannot be defined at all. A war the purpose of which is essentially defensive has customarily been regarded as a war that leaves the power and vital interests of the enemy substantially unchanged. In a still broader sense, a defensive war is one that is compatible with the international order existing at the outbreak of hostilities, or one even fought to preserve that order.

In the American doctrine, however, a war fought for professedly defensive purposes is not equated with a war designed to preserve the *status quo*. This doctrine may have a *status quo* orientation with respect to the deliberate resort to force as an instrument for effecting change. Yet it clearly does not have this same bias once force is employed in "defense" against aggression. The moral law may be interpreted as forbidding change, if such change implies the resort to force as an instrument of national policy. But once force is employed in defense against aggression, the same moral law apparently sanctions force as an instrument for effecting the most drastic change. The result appears paradoxical. A doctrine that forbids the resort to force even in circumstances calculated to preserve international order nevertheless permits force to be employed "defensively" in such a manner that the result may well be to destroy that order.

Nevertheless, what must appear paradoxical and inconsistent when judged according to the traditional nature and purposes of a defensive war assumes a remarkable clarity and consistency when the purposes of defense are once identified with prevention or deterrence. The American doctrine accepts as obvious the equation of the purposes of defense with the purposes of deterrence. The moral justification of the former must therefore provide the moral justification of the latter. "We are convinced," Secretary Acheson declared in explaining the deterrent and consequently the defensive purpose of the North Atlantic Treaty, "that we can best contribute to the maintenance of peace by joining with other nations in making it absolutely clear in advance that any armed attack affecting our national security would be met with overwhelming force." [59]

What was it, Mr. Dulles asked shortly before becoming Secretary of State, that had kept the Red armies from over-running all of Europe and Asia? "The most reasonable explanation is that the rulers of Russia knew that if they indulged in this open aggression in any area of vital concern to the United States or which by treaty we were bound to defend, their sources and means of power in Russia would have been visited with incredible destruction." [60] And if the potential aggressor had been restrained for this reason, did we not want more of it? If there is the capability and the will to respond to aggression with overwhelming or at the very least with punishing force, and that will is clearly manifested, the likelihood that potential aggressors will choose the path of violence can be reduced to a vanishing point.

"The essential thing is that a potential aggressor should know in advance that he can and will be made to suffer for his aggression more than he can possibly gain by it . . . a prospective attacker is not likely to invade if he believes the probable hurt will outbalance the probable gain." [61] In these words Secretary Dulles laid down the necessary conditions for deterrence, as well as the assumed consequences of that policy. Yet in so doing, Mr. Dulles did no more than

[59] Press Statement, January 26, 1949 (*Bulletin*, xx, 160). The Acheson statement was a paraphrase of the statement made by President Truman in his January 20, 1949 inaugural address: "If we can make it sufficiently clear, in advance, that any armed attack affecting our national security would be met with overwhelming force, the armed attack might never occur."

[60] Address to Advertising Council, Detroit, Mich., November 27, 1951 (*Bulletin*, xxv[2], 940).

[61] John Foster Dulles, "Policy for Security and Peace," pp. 358-59.

generalize the reflections and beliefs of his predecessors.[62] The claim of novelty, made curiously enough both by Mr. Dulles' supporters and by many of his critics, was entirely without foundation. If deterrence constituted, as Secretary Dulles was later to insist, "one of the great advances of our time," it was an advance that in principle could be identified neither with party nor with administration.[63]

Thus, while deterrence has been regarded as serving only a defensive purpose, it has also appeared as a radically improved version of traditional notions of defense—an improved version because a policy of deterrence is concentrated upon the attempt to insure that peace-loving nations may realize the purposes otherwise frequently realized only through a defensive war though without ever having to engage in such a war. It is precisely this latter feature which has appeared

---

[62] Thus President Truman declared in his 1952 State of the Union message: "Our objective is to have a well-equipped, active defense force large enough—in concert with the forces of our allies—to deter aggression and to inflict punishing losses on the enemy immediately if we should be attacked." (*Bulletin*, xxvi[1], 82.)   An endless number of expressions of deterrence, against which the Dulles formulation seems no more than a paraphrase, can be found for the years 1948-52.

[63] It is only fair to note that Mr. Dulles never advanced the claim of novelty for the strategy of deterrence. Quite to the contrary, on numerous occasions he acknowledged that the policy of the Truman administration—apart from several "lapses," and notably Korea—had also been based upon the principle of deterrence. Thus the North Atlantic Treaty was from the start expressly founded upon a deterrent strategy, and one which threatened the potential aggressor with the most extreme measures of retaliation. What Mr. Dulles did claim was to have carried the principle of deterrence several steps beyond the point at which his predecessors had left it, principally by taking advantage of the opportunities supposedly offered by the new weaponry which formed the core of America's mobile retaliatory power. The essence of the Dulles claim, therefore, was that by so doing he had given deterrence its most effective and "logical" application. On the other hand, the Dulles critics insisted, for the most part, that in seeking to apply deterrence in areas and in circumstances of the most varied character, and in relying to an ever-increasing degree upon nuclear weapons, the Eisenhower-Dulles policy had misapplied that principle and had deprived it of the essential quality of credibility.

to lend credence to the claim that deterrence is something new under the sun. For the principal object of deterrence is not merely to reduce the probability of war by making clear to potential aggressors that any future resort to armed force would be resisted. To so describe deterrence is indeed to reduce it to little more than traditional notions of defense, whereas its central and decisive purpose is to banish force altogether from history. By comparison, the much more modest purposes implicit in traditional notions of defense must appear trifling.

Nevertheless, if the quality of novelty is claimed on behalf of deterrence, that claim can be validated only on the level of policy, not doctrine. On the level of policy, there is a world of difference between the endeavor to do away with violence in the relations of states by promoting treaties that "outlaw" war as an instrument of national policy and the attempt to prevent armed aggression by threatening potential aggressors with annihilation or severe punishment should they seek to carry out their designs. On the level of doctrine, however, both policies spring from the conviction that violence is not an inevitable evil in a society of sovereign states, that the resort to force is instead an entirely avoidable means for effecting change or for resolving conflicting interests. This being so, it is the prevention of war rather than its mere limitation that must form the great object of policy. The Kellogg-Briand Pact and nuclear deterrence may represent radically disparate means for pursuing this objective, but both policies spring from the same basic aspiration. If war cannot be exorcized by the conclusion of multilateral treaties solemnly invoking that purpose, the prevention of war must be sought by insuring that the reaction to aggression is made sufficiently punishing to leave no potential aggressor in doubt that he would lose far more than he could possibly hope to gain by resorting to aggression.

Whatever the specific form deterrence has taken, as far

as its doctrinal basis is concerned it is cut from the same cloth and is informed by the same basic purpose. To be sure, in its unlimited version deterrence is a literal application of what can be termed the "pure theory of prevention" in intending to banish aggression altogether by threatening potential aggressors with total destruction.[64] Yet in its limited or graduated form as well, deterrence pursues the same objective: it still intends to exorcise the evil of aggression, not by threatening potential aggressors with total destruction but by convincing them, if need be through action, that aggression is no longer a paying adventure. Limited deterrence, then, differs from total deterrence in that it believes, however reluctantly, in the possibility of redeeming not only potential aggressors but actual aggressors as well. Instead of endeavoring to reform would-be aggressors simply by threatening them with annihilation, limited deterrence hopes to accomplish the same purpose, if possible, by threatening potential aggressors with severe punishment, and if necessary, by carrying out this threat against actual aggressors.

Is deterrence then simply an improved version of traditional concepts of defense? Are there no moral issues raised by the former that have not already been raised by the latter? Is the moral justification for deterrence substantially identical

[64] A rather folksy, though an essentially accurate, definition of the end sought by pure deterrence was recently given by the Commander of the Strategic Air Command. "Our real mission," General Power declared in testifying before the House Appropriations Subcommittee, "is to have that Russian planner get up from his table every morning and turn to Mr. Khrushchev and shake his head and say, 'Today is not the day, Comrade.'" (House Subcommittee of the Committee on Appropriations Hearings, *Department of Defense Appropriations for 1960* [86th Cong., 1st Sess.], Part II, p. 380.) General Power noted that this mission could be insured only if the deterrent threat were based upon a margin of striking force so great that "even an idiot would know that, if he attacks this country, he would be literally and figuratively destroyed" (p. 375). The same reasoning must presumably hold for those areas considered vital to American security.

with the justification for defense? How one answers these questions must depend largely upon the degree of success that a policy of deterrence enjoys. For the paradox of deterrence is that it is defensive—or perhaps even less than defensive—as long as the need to employ force does not arise and almost inevitably more than defensive once the necessity for employing force does arise. This may be apparent when the deterrent threat assumes an extreme or unlimited form. It is equally true, though perhaps not so readily apparent, when the deterrent threat assumes a "limited" form. What, indeed, are the limits to limited deterrence? That question has yet to be answered with clarity, and not without reason. A war which is fought not simply to prevent an aggressor from achieving his immediate aims but also to prevent future aggression and to insure that the present aggressor will alter his habits in the future, can have no clearly defined or readily discernible limits.

It may nevertheless be argued that there is still a vital difference between a war waged to destroy an aggressor and a war waged to reform an aggressor by convincing him that further aggression must prove unprofitable. The latter purpose presumably requires only that the force employed be sufficient both to defend and to punish, and thereby to deter aggression in the future. But how vital is this difference? When is an aggressor sufficiently punished so as to learn his lesson? It is not for nothing that a doctrine so strongly committed to making the punishment fit the crime has nevertheless remained silent on the nature and limits of punishment.

However much limited deterrence speaks of changing the disposition of the aggressor, once engaged in hostilities it is not the aggressor's disposition to engage in future aggression but his power to do so that must be changed. A "punishing war" which nevertheless leaves the power of the aggressor substantially intact can provide no real assurance that the aggressor will be deterred from renewing his aggressions in the future, perhaps with even greater determination. Aggressors may indeed cease to be aggressive if they are shown that aggression is unprofitable, even though their power to commit further aggression is left intact. But if history is to prove of any use in this matter, it is equally clear that aggressors may not cease to be aggressive in such circumstances. At any rate, the assurance deterrence seeks cannot be satisfied simply by a temporary change in the disposition of the injured aggressor. That assurance can be secured only by a change in the aggressor's intentions and power. It is for this reason that the degree of force required to insure against future aggression has no readily discernible limits. The very logic of a war fought for this purpose must tend to convert it almost imperceptibly from a war whose intent is merely to punish an aggressor into a war whose end becomes the complete destruction of the power of the aggressor. If it is nevertheless asserted that a war fought to vindicate the principle of "limited" deterrence must be regarded as having a strictly defensive purpose, then there remain virtually no limits to the concrete objectives that may be sought by those waging an allegedly defensive war.[65]

[65] It is ironic that a doctrine which so emphatically rejects the initiation of force for preventive purposes, is so insistent upon pursuing just such purposes once force is undertaken in defense against aggression. A policy of resorting to preventive war is absolutely condemned, among other reasons, because it allegedly assumes the inevitability of conflict and thereby must presumably depend upon an omniscience to know the future that is denied to man. In fact, however, the argument for preventive war does not depend upon any claim to omniscience in reading the future. That argument proceeds, as all statecraft must proceed, upon an estimate of the future to which a varying degree of probability may be attached. It is obviously true, though, that a policy of preventive war does have the intent to "determine"— some may prefer the term "prejudice"—the future. But if preventive war is to be morally condemned for the latter reason, then it is difficult to see why the same judgment may not be made with respect to a policy that employs force—even though initially in defense—for predominantly preventive purposes. Indeed, it does not seem unreasonable to insist that in

If the purposes of deterrence are more than merely defensive, to what extent may they be regarded as having a punitive or retributive character? It is of course true that the "punishment" a policy of deterrence holds out against aggressors is expressly interpreted as serving primarily a preventive purpose. Yet the intent to find in the measures threatened by deterrence a strictly punitive purpose as well, cannot be—and indeed is not—specifically disclaimed, particularly with respect to the wrongdoer who resorted to aggression and whose exclusive moral and legal responsibility for initiating hostilities is assumed as a matter of faith. The distinction drawn between the evil aggressor and the innocent population of the aggressor state nevertheless requires that a limit be set to the purpose of retribution. Since the responsibility for aggression cannot be imputed to the innocent masses, insofar as the measures taken in war affect not only the aggressor but the innocent they cannot easily be given a punitive interpretation.[66]

the nuclear age it is not the resort to force which most seriously "prejudices" the future but the manner in which force is employed—whether defensively or offensively.

[66] The picture of a world divided into the evil few and the innocent many may become blurred by the passions engendered during a period of war, but it has never been erased. Even a policy of unconditional surrender must somehow be adjusted to it. During World War II President Roosevelt took care to emphasize on more than one occasion that: "In our uncompromising policy [i.e., unconditional surrender] we mean no harm to the common people of the Axis nations. But we do mean to impose punishment and retribution in full upon their guilty, barbaric leaders." (*Bulletin*, VIII, 146.) And in the war crimes trials that followed the war, American tribunals consistently professed this distinction. Thus, in one of the post-Nuremberg proceedings dealing with those accused of crimes against peace the court declared: "The defendants now before us were neither high public officials in the civil government nor high military officers. Their participation was that of followers and not leaders. If we lower the standard of participation to include them, it is difficult to find a logical place to draw the line between the guilty and the innocent among the great mass of the German people. It is, of course, unthinkable that the majority of Germans should be condemned as guilty of committing crimes against peace. This would amount

Although the purpose of war in the American doctrine admittedly partakes of a punitive character, care is taken to set limits to the retributive element and to lay primary emphasis upon the preventive purpose of war once it is undertaken in defense against aggression. But the distinction drawn between a war whose purpose is primarily preventive and a war whose purpose is primarily retributive is not an obvious one. That distinction cannot rest simply upon the intent a belligerent ascribes to his behavior, but must surely depend to an even larger degree upon the nature of this behavior. As far as actual behavior is concerned, the uncertain limits of a war fought expressly for deterrent or preventive purposes must make it very difficult at best to distinguish it from a war whose dominating purpose is in fact retributive. Nor is it without significance that the most effective measure of prevention in war is also the most characteristic measure of retribution, the extermination of the enemy. And even if the intent informing the purpose of prevention could be clearly distinguished from the intent

to a determination of collective guilt to which the corollary of mass punishment is the logical result, for which there is no precedent in international law and no justification in human relations." *The I. G. Farben Trial, Law Reports of Trials of War Criminals*, x (1949), 39. Given this distinction, the measures taken in war which affect the "common people" of the aggressor state cannot be accorded a punitive interpretation—they are not "acts of punishment" but acts which, however unfortunate in their "incidental" effects, are made "militarily necessary" in order to defeat and to punish the true aggressor. Observers have been inclined, for the most part, to attribute this picture of a world divided between the evil few and the many good to our belief in the inherent goodness of man and the inevitability of human progress. Perhaps of equal significance, however, is a much simpler though somewhat less complimentary explanation, i.e., the exception to date of the American continent from the ravages of modern war. Whether the attitude we have heretofore manifested in war could survive in hostilities carried directly to American territory remains to be seen. Elmer Davis once ventured the opinion that "if a few Russian atomic bombs were dropped on American cities, I doubt if our statesmen would find it advisable to say anything more about how we love the Russian people." "Vox Populi and Foreign Policy," *Harper's*, June, 1952, p. 72.

informing the purpose of retribution, how relevant is this distinction if the concrete results issuing from these two purposes are indistinguishable? A Carthaginian policy is, after all, a matter of action, not of intent.

The American doctrine of the just war may purport to place narrow limits upon the circumstances in which states may legitimately resort to force. But it is difficult not to conclude that this doctrine places almost no substantive limits upon the specific objectives which may legitimately be sought once force is employed in defense against aggression. It is not that the American doctrine condones the avowal of any and all purposes in a war waged against aggression, but rather that the purposes it does avow—defense and peace—set no meaningful limitations to the specific objectives that may be pursued in war. The frequent contention that in the American doctrine war is not an instrument of policy but an end in itself is therefore misleading. If war cannot deliberately be chosen as an instrument of national policy, once war has been thrust upon peace-loving nations they may employ force for achieving almost any results. Accordingly, force may be justified as an instrument for achieving almost any policy.

V

If the American doctrine of the just war assumes a necessary relationship between the justice of resorting to war and the purposes sought in war, it also assumes a similar relationship between the causes and purposes of war and the manner of employing force. The same principles of the moral law that sanction the resort to war and the purposes sought in war also sanction the manner in which force is employed. From this point of view at least, war is not the solvent of all moral distinctions.

This is not to suggest the irrelevance for American doctrine of the distinction drawn between the "ethics of war" and the ethics of peace. Obviously, this distinction has been significant for doctrine and indeed may be related to the belief that the manner of employing force receives its moral justification from the circumstances attending the initiation of force and the purposes sought in war. If the ethics of peace are held to condemn the principle that the end justifies the means, the ethics of war are held to endorse that principle. Thus the ethics of peace must condemn the resort to preventive war, however desirable the ends sought through such a war. But the ethics of war may justify the use of almost any weapons and the employment of any methods which realize the ends or purposes of the just war.[67]

Nevertheless, moral complacency over the manner of employing force does not stem primarily from the conviction that the procedures of war fall beyond the moral pale—that the ethics of war know nothing of the ethics of peace—but from the belief that the justification for these procedures has been clearly resolved. Hence, if the problems incurred in devising the most effective means for deterring or resisting aggression are frequently seen as involving only "technical" questions, this is to be explained by the belief that only technical questions remain to be resolved. Moral indifference is thus the result of moral certainty.[68]

[67] James B. Conant has given a typical expression of this distinction in declaring that "while liberty has repeatedly been gained by war, once won it can be protected only by adherence to those moral principles which were repudiated in its achievement. . . . If we become sufficiently oppressed by the logical inconsistency of our emphasis on the distinction between war and peace, we might repudiate the paradox by accepting the premise of the totalitarians that at all times the end justifies the means. Once we had gone over to their position, the doctrine of a preventive war . . . would be quite compatible with the philosophy of the nation." "Force and Freedom," *The Atlantic Monthly*, January, 1949, pp. 19-21.

[68] The editors of *Time* were only pursuing this doctrine to its logical end in finding "no moral problem in the H-bomb that was not present in the

To be sure, moral indifference to the manner of employing force may not be due simply to moral certitude respecting the causes of, and the purposes sought in, war. This indifference may also stem from the conviction that once force is employed man has moved from the realm of freedom to a world of necessity. "When you resorted to force as the arbiter of human difficulty," President Eisenhower has pointed out in articulating this conviction, "you didn't know where you were going. . . . If you got deeper and deeper, there was just no limit except what was imposed by the limitations of force iself."[69] There is, of course, nothing novel in the view that war pursues a logic of its own over which the participants can have at best only a marginal influence. And for reasons which must be readily apparent, this view has never seemed more influential than at present, nor its consequences more threatening. If war must follow a necessity of its own, then it is useless to indulge in moral judgments on the manner in which hostilities are conducted. If war has no limitations save those imposed "by the limitations of force itself," then the attempt to distinguish among the weapons and methods of warfare, let alone to observe such distinctions, is little more than a futile gesture. Moral distinctions, and moral judgments based on these distinctions, are largely irrelevant once men have decided to make force the arbiter of their differences.[70]

A-bomb, none in the A-bomb that was not present in the mass bombing of cities, none of these that is not present in war itself, and no grave problems in war that are not present in the basic question of the permissibility of force in any circumstances." *Time*, April 12, 1954, p. 33.

[69] Remarks made at press conference, January 12, 1955 (*New York Times*, January 13, 1955) .

[70] The curious consequences of this view were illuminated with a rare clarity in the AEC hearings *In the Matter of J. Robert Oppenheimer* (Atomic Energy Commission, 1954) . However compelling other considerations were in the decision to make an all-out effort to develop the hydrogen bomb, it would have been incredible if those involved in the decision had not been influenced by moral conviction as well. Yet the significant point

There is, at least, a kind of consistency in the view that assumes a determination both with respect to the institution of war itself and with respect to the conduct of war, though this is perhaps all one may say for this view. In fact, however, earlier ages were not so consistent. Although accepting force as an inevitable concomitant of a society of sovereign states, the attempt was nevertheless made to limit the role of force. The institution of war may have been seen as a necessary evil. But man must still address his efforts to limiting the functions served by force and the effects of force upon society. It is this view that was instrumental in leading to the limiting of war's conduct and, of course, of the ends sought in war. The presuppositions upon which the American doctrine rests do not even have the virtue of simple consistency, however, since a markedly voluntaristic interpretation of war itself has been juxtaposed with a

that emerges from the testimony is the extent to which many sought to deny that they were so influenced. No doubt this denial stemmed in part from an assumption which equated moral opposition to making the hydrogen bomb with opposition to American policy as a whole vis-à-vis the Soviet Union. In large part, however, it is clear that this denial stemmed from the conviction that moral distinctions and moral judgments were somehow irrelevant in such matters and served only to reflect a lack of realism. Thus in responding to the question of whether he had opposed the hydrogen bomb on moral grounds, George Kennan declared: ". . . I didn't consider that. After all, we are dealing with weapons here, and when you are dealing with weapons you are dealing with things to kill people, and I don't think the considerations of morality are relevant. I had real worries . . . about the effects of this on our future policy and suitability of our future policy" (p. 368). Five years later Mr. Kennan was to write: "But that we cannot rule out force completely in international affairs does not seem to me to constitute a reason for being indifferent to the ways in which force is applied—to the moral implications of weapons and their uses. It is true that all distinctions among weapons from the moral standpoint are relative and arbitrary. . . . But who is to say that relative distinctions are not meaningful? I cannot help feeling that the weapon of indiscriminate mass destruction goes farther than anything the Christian ethic can properly accept." "Foreign Policy and Christian Conscience," *Atlantic Monthly,* May, 1959, pp. 47-48.

markedly deterministic interpretation of war's conduct. Still, this inconsistency has its own logic, and it is not without significance that as a general rule the greater the voluntarism shown toward war, the greater the determinism shown toward war's conduct. For there is a direct and obvious link between the optimism which assumes that force can be banished from history and the pessimism which concludes that if the achievement of this end should prove impossible, it will prove equally impossible to set any meaningful limitations on war's conduct. Thus in recent years those who have professed the greatest faith in a policy of nuclear deterrence as the means for exorcizing force from history have unfailingly insisted almost in the same breath that should nuclear deterrence somehow fail it will prove impossible to set any meaningful limitations on war's conduct. Freedom from war is therefore made dependent upon the appreciation of the necessity of war's unlimited effects.

Given this logic, the conclusion is inescapable. The central if not the sole moral problem must be war itself and not its methods.[71] The lesson that total war teaches is not that nations must exercise restraint in war as in peace but

[71] The statement in the text is a paraphrase of Henry Stimson's remark in 1947 that "we as well as our enemies have contributed to the proof that the central moral problem is war and not its methods, and that a continuance of war will in all probability end with the destruction of our civilization." "Nuremberg: Landmark in Law," *Foreign Affairs*, xxv (January, 1947), 189. In his now famous account of the decision to drop the atomic bomb on Hiroshima and Nagasaki, Mr. Stimson brings the same point out in even sharper relief. "In this last great action of the Second World War we were given final proof that war is death. War in the twentieth century has grown steadily more barbarous, more destructive, more debased in all its aspects. Now, with the release of atomic energy, man's ability to destroy himself is very nearly complete. The bombs dropped on Hiroshima and Nagasaki ended a war. They also made it wholly clear that we must never have another war. This is the lesson men and leaders everywhere must learn, and I believe that when they learn it they will find a way to lasting peace. There is no other choice." *On Active Service in Peace and War*, p. 633. But perhaps the most striking recent expression of the view discussed in the

that there must never be another war. "We can't stand another global war," President Truman declared in one of his first major addresses as President, "we can't ever have another war, unless it is total war, and that means the end of our civilization as we know it."[72] Seven years later, in his last State of the Union address and presumably with the benefit of hindsight on the Korean experience, Mr. Truman returned to the same theme. "The war of the future would be one in which man could extinguish millions of lives at one blow, demolish the great cities of the world, wipe out the cultural achievements of the past—and destroy the very structure of a civilization that has been slowly and painfully built up through hundreds of generations. Such a war is not a possible policy for rational men."[73] President Eisenhower has consistently expressed similar opinions with still greater fervency.

This is not to suggest, however, that in the doctrine it professes this nation has sought to deny the continued

text has been given by a distinguished European statesman. "I must . . . say that the proposal to humanize war has always struck me as hypocrisy. I have difficulty in seeing the difference from a moral and humane point of view between the use of a guided missile of great power which can kill tens and even hundreds of people without regard for age or sex, and which if used repeatedly will kill millions, and the use of an atomic bomb which achieves the same result at the first stroke. Does crime against humanity begin only at the moment when a certain number of innocent people are killed or at the moment when the first one is killed?" Paul-Henri Spaak, "The Atom Bomb and NATO," *Foreign Affairs*, xxxiii (April, 1955) , 355. The answer to M. Spaak's question can be given in one word: both. Of course, M. Spaak is not so perverse as seriously to suggest that the killing of the first person in war is as great a crime against humanity as the indiscriminate slaughter of millions. He has simply assumed that whatever the weapons and methods employed in war the ultimate consequences will necessarily be the same. Given this assumption—erroneous to be sure—his charge of hypocrisy is as unexceptionable as his conclusion: "What seems really criminal to me is the idea of having recourse to war whatever form it might take. . . ."

[72] Address, October 7, 1945 (*Bulletin,* xiii, 558) .

[73] State of the Union address, January 7, 1953 (*Bulletin,* xxviii, 95) .

validity even in war of what are conceived as the "imperative requirements of humanity." On the contrary, in its treatment of prisoners of war and of occupied populations few nations have shown greater sensitivity to these requirements.[74] But the critical point is that the restraints to be observed in war have been identified almost entirely with the protection and treatment of the victims of war. Both in doctrine and in practice, the absence of attempts to place substantive restraints upon the actual conduct of hostilities stands in striking contrast to "humanitarian" restraints which must be observed in the treatment of victims of war. Whereas the hostile measures taken against the collective "aggressor" raise only technical questions to be resolved in the most expedient and economical manner, the treatment of enemy individuals who have fallen within our control must clearly be governed by the requirements of humanity and the respect for fundamental human rights. Thus we have been as insistent upon further strengthening the protection to be given the victims of war (for example, our role in the 1949 Geneva Conventions on the Protection of the Victims of War) as we have been resistant to finding substantive limitations upon the actual conduct of hostilities.[75]

[74] Though it is probably true that our magnanimity as a nation toward the enemy who has once fallen under our control must be attributed in part to our having so far escaped the ravages of invasion or direct attack. On the other side, it is also clear that past good fortune in war has materially contributed to the abandon we have shown in the actual conduct of hostilities. B. H. Liddell-Hart makes much the same point with respect to Great Britain. In tracing the British use of air power in World War II to habits acquired from traditional naval strategy, Liddell-Hart observes: "In the actual treatment of persons on the opposing side the British habit has been more humane than most, helped by the relative degree of dispassionateness that was fostered by prolonged freedom from the ravages of invasion. On the other hand, the circumstances naturally encouraged a more ruthless type of strategy in dealing with the enemy collectively and striking at his property." *The Revolution in Warfare* (1947), p. 89.

[75] Indeed, the remarkable solicitude we have manifested toward the treatment rendered the victims of war found an almost utopian expression in

This curious ambivalence is rooted in a long-standing controversy over the nature and purpose of the restraints to be applied in war. In the history of the attempts to impose limitations on the conduct of war two views have vied with one another. The one, and much the older, view has placed primary emphasis upon the regulation and direction of actual hostilities. It assumes that war is not, or at least need not and should not be, the negation of all order, but rather a method for effecting change within an order whose principal units are sovereign nations. War may be a very grim and tragic "game," but it must nevertheless remain a game, in the sense that the participants accept limitations upon their behavior, if it is to prove at all compatible with order. The principal purpose for restraining the manner in which hostilities are conducted is not to protect human rights or to mitigate suffering but to insure that the minimum foundations of order will be preserved even in war. And since the international order is an order made up of states, these restraints must seek to prevent a war waged in such a manner as to threaten the very existence of the participants, thereby striking at the foundations upon which any international order must rest. Admittedly, the view that violence can and must be regulated, that it can and must somehow be rendered compatible with order, suggests a paradox of no small proportion. Yet paradoxical as it may seem, it is only in this manner that the minimal requirements of order can be uneasily reconciled with an institution so apparently inimical to order. In a world in which order among nations, however minimal, is imperative, but in which

many of the provisions of the 1949 Geneva Convention Relative to the Protection of Civilian Persons in Time of War. The rather grimly facetious suggestion has therefore been made that in view of the far-reaching restrictions laid upon occupation authorities in the 1949 Geneva Convention the only problem that remains to be solved in wars of the future concerns the possible means of becoming a "protected" victim of war.

war has so far proven unavoidable, there has appeared no other alternative.[76]

The other and more modern view implicitly rejects the contention that war can or should be regarded as an institution compatible with some form of order. In this view, the essence of war is that it signifies the breakdown of all order. The restraints that are applicable during a period of hostilities can only have as their purpose the mitigation of human suffering and the protection of those fundamental human rights which survive even in war. It is not their purpose to regulate the manner in which a game may be played, a game in which the principal participants are sovereign states and the principal objectives are power and prestige.[77] Besides, if the aggressive resort to war is both immoral and illegal, the aggressor as such can no longer be considered as endowed with any rights—not even the right to continued existence. Hence, the purpose of restraints as applied to the manner of employing force is not to protect any rights or legitimate interests of the aggressor but to

[76] In Herbert Butterfield's *Christianity, Diplomacy and War* (1953), may be found one of the few contemporary expressions of the above view. "In a world where we cannot eliminate war, how can we control it, and how can we maintain an international order still?" (p. 25). ". . . one might as well face the fact that so long as an international order exists—or so long as we might desire one to exist—wars must come short of the last degree of irreconciliability and retain some of the characteristics of a conflict between potential allies, some trace of the fact that they are quarrels between friends" (p. 97).

[77] Thus a recent, and typical, expression of this view reads: "We shall utterly fail to understand the true character of the law of war unless we realize that its purpose is almost entirely humanitarian in the literal sense of the word, namely, to prevent or mitigate suffering and, in some cases, to rescue life from the savagery of battle and passion. This, and not the regulation and direction of hostilities, is its essential purpose. Rules of warfare are not primarily rules governing the technicalities and artifices of a game. They have evolved or have been expressly enacted for the protection of actual or potential victims of war." H. Lauterpacht, "The Problem of the Revision of the Law of War," *British Yearbook of International Law*, XXIX (1952), 363-64.

protect the inherent rights of individuals *qua* individuals.

In contrasting these two views it is misleading to suggest that the former is somehow unconcerned with or inimical to humanitarian considerations. It is apparent, however, that the former view is predominantly political in character, in that its first concern is with the task of attempting to preserve at least some semblance of international order even in war. Consequently, the distinctly humanitarian purpose of the restraints introduced in war forms a secondary consideration. The latter view, in concentrating its attention almost exclusively on the humanitarian purpose of these restraints, is necessarily unconcerned with the distinctly political problem. War may prove completely destructive of the political order existing at the time of the initiation of hostilities, but the requirements of humanity are alleged to remain as imperative and as unyielding in a war fought to unconditional surrender and the complete destruction of the "aggressor" as in a war fought to adjust a frontier.

Nevertheless, the significant issue between these two views is not simply that the one is concerned primarily with preserving even in war the conditions necessary for the survival of the participants, whereas the other is concerned only with preserving the conditions necessary for the observance of fundamental human rights. Instead, the critical issue is which view offers the most hopeful prospect for reconciling the fact of war with the least possible destruction of human rights. The position that insists upon the almost exclusively humanitarian nature and purpose of the restraints introduced in war will not clearly face up to this difficult task of somehow reconciling the fact of violence with the demands of humanity. To do so would necessarily involve it in an inquiry into the political conditions which make the effectiveness of "purely" humanitarian restraints at all possible. Such an inquiry into matters political would not only taint its scheme of interpretation, but would challenge, if not wholly shatter, its absurd and sentimental assumption that the preservation of the sovereign requirements of humanity is a problem that transcends politics and is independent of any need to preserve the sovereign requirements of that "metaphysical entity," the state. Such an inquiry could not help but demonstrate one of the clearest of all historical lessons—that in order to mitigate human suffering and to reduce the savagery of war, the attempt must first be made to render war compatible with some semblance of order, and that this can only mean an order among states. Nor could it avoid the conclusion that the essential condition for the observance of distinctively human rights in war is the continued observance among the belligerents of the rights of states, and that during war these rights can only be observed if there is a mutual acceptance of inhibitions on the actual conduct of hostilities.

If the American doctrine finds an almost purely humanitarian purpose in the restraints imposed in war, and equates these restraints largely with the treatment to be accorded the victims of war, it nevertheless does not deny the desirability of setting some limits to the weapons and methods employed in the actual conduct of hostilities. To be sure, this doctrine does not acknowledge an equality, moral or legal, between the aggressor and those fighting a war of defense against aggression.[78] War is no game played for

[78] For this reason, as Secretary Dulles pointed out, the principle of neutrality "which pretends that a nation can best gain safety for itself by being indifferent to the fate of others" is not only short-sighted but immoral—for it means "conniving at aggression." Although Mr. Dulles' critics have made much of his utterances on neutrality, the excessive form in which these statements were frequently cast ought not to obscure the point that contemporary American doctrine does equate neutrality (in a just war) with indifference and the latter with immorality and the absence of "community feeling." Yet the indifference that characterized the traditional institution of neutrality did not reflect the absence of "community feeling." The indifference of neutrals toward the outcome of war proved possible only because the solidarity of the international society was

such cynical objectives as power and prestige, and one in which the participants can claim an equal status. The aggressor is not looked upon simply as another player, entitled to insist upon the observance of rules which set limits to the punishment he may receive at the hands of his opponents. Those states waging a defensive war enjoy a superior moral and legal position and are thereby entitled to respond to aggression in places and with means of their own choosing; hence, their problem in responding to aggression is first and foremost a technical problem, not a moral problem. Still, the manner of employing force is not regarded as free from any moral or legal restraint. Although the aggressor must be defeated, and although peace-loving nations have a right and even a duty to deal with an aggressor so as to insure that he will have neither the inclination nor the ability to pursue his evil design in the future, no more destruction and suffering ought to be inflicted than the necessities of war require. The employment of any kind or degree of force unnecessary for the purpose (s) of war and needlessly causing human suffering and physical destruction therefore stands condemned. And since a clear distinction is drawn by doctrine between the evil aggressor and the innocent population of the aggressor state, the obligation to employ force in as discriminating a manner as the necessities of war permit must also appear compelling. In consequence, the noncombatant population of an aggressor state ought not

---

sufficiently great, even in war, as not to make the outcome of a conflict a matter of deep concern to the nonparticipants. The disappearance of neutrality was not the result of a growing sense of community but almost the precise opposite, as a comparison between the experiences of the nineteenth and twentieth centuries will reveal. Equally misplaced are contemporary interpretations which find in the traditional institution of neutrality an indifference between right and wrong. To so interpret the wars of an earlier era is to impute to these conflicts a significance that would have escaped the comprehension of both the participants and the nonparticipants.

to be made the direct and deliberate object of attack and should be spared from injuries not incidental to military operations directed against combatant forces and other legitimate military objectives.

The American doctrine thus acknowledges that even in a war waged against an aggressor there ought to be certain restraints placed on the manner in which force may be employed. In a period marked by constant change in the weapons and methods of war, this doctrine insists upon the continued validity of the so-called general principles of the law of war in their application to the actual conduct of hostilities. Yet the difficulties that attend this insistence must be readily apparent, and they cannot but give rise to skepticism, if not with respect to the very sincerity of this profession, then at least with respect to its practical effect. A commitment to restrain the manner in which force is employed by a readiness to observe the general principle of humanity is not altogether impressive when accompanied by the conviction that war has no limitations save those imposed by the limitations of force itself. Nor can this commitment appear very impressive when placed alongside the belief that the central moral problem is war itself and not the weapons and methods of war, and that in the manner of responding to aggression the principal problems for peace-loving states waging a defensive war are technical rather than moral in character.

These considerations apart, the simple commitment to restrain the manner of employing force so as to conform to the general principle of humanity has never proven to be very effective in placing meaningful limitations upon the conduct of hostilities. It must prove even less effective today. The principle of humanity in war and the concomitant principle of military necessity have always depended for their effective operation upon standards that are neither self-evident nor immutable. As applied to novel weapons and methods of war, the principle of humanity can be used, if at all, to determine the legitimacy of employing such weapons or methods only in terms of their military necessity. But even if it is assumed that the purposes of war remain constant, it has never been easy to determine whether a specific weapon or method does cause unnecessary suffering or physical destruction when judged in terms of the purposes for which war is waged.

Nor is the fundamental ambiguity and consequent uncertainty which mark the interpretation of this principle alleviated by reference to the actual practice of states. For it is precisely the variation in state practice, reflecting a variation in interpretation, that has accentuated the ambiguity and uncertainty already inherent in the principle of humanity. Thus, in both doctrine and practice this nation has always assumed the validity of its own peculiar interpretation of the demands imposed by the principle of humanity. Perhaps more markedly than with other nations, that principle has been interpreted as having its principal application to those who must apply it and thence radiating outward with sharply decreasing intensity. With us the principle of humanity "begins at home" and comes very close to staying at home, at least as far as the actual conduct of hostilities is concerned. For this reason, we have always been disposed to interpret the "needless or unnecessary" suffering condemned by the principle of humanity largely as a moral sanction for measures whose purpose is designed to save American lives, whatever other effects they may have.

"If it is preferable to engage in a war of attrition, one American life for one enemy life," declared the Secretary of the Air Force at the outset of the cold war, "then we are wrong. That is not our way." [79] More recently, the com-

---

[79] Statement of Stuart Symington, House Committee on Armed Services Hearings, *The National Defense Program—Unification and Strategy* (81st Cong., 1st Sess.) , pp. 402-03.

manding general of the Strategic Air Command complained against those who have advocated using only conventional bombs in any war other than a "little tiny police action." ". . . I have a deep moral sense as it applies to Americans," General Power declared, "and I get a little indignant with people who become very lofty in their thinking and do not want to kill a few of the enemy but would gladly risk additional American lives. My crews are more important to me than the enemy." [80]

These may be unusually candid expressions of a conviction that is better left unsaid. But it would be rash to assume that they represent no more than an isolated view. However significant the economic attractions of the Eisenhower administration's policy of placing an ever greater reliance upon the threat of nuclear retaliation for deterring aggression, a further attraction—at least until 1956—was undoubtedly the concern it professed to have for the saving of American lives in the event of war. What Secretary Dulles justified in terms of the dictates of the moral law, General Power justified in terms of his "deep moral sense as it applies to Americans." The latter formulation may be less discrete, but that is perhaps the only difference. Whether the measures to which this conviction leads may nevertheless be considered morally commendable on other grounds than the principle of humanity in war is beside the point. What is relevant here is the observation that even as an interpretation of the principle of humanity, this conviction cannot easily be regarded as a perversion of that principle's true intent, in view of the vague criteria upon which the principle of humanity must depend and has always depended for its interpretation. [81]

[80] House Subcommittee of the Committee on Appropriations Hearings, *Department of Defense Appropriations, 1960* (86th Cong., 1st Sess.) , Part II, p. 388.

[81] Of course, if the application of the principle of humanity in war were to be judged simply by the concern shown for the "other" as well as for

Still more significant in this respect is the consideration that the relevance of invoking the principle of humanity cannot be usefully considered apart from the purposes for which war is waged. A war fought for the limited purpose of obtaining a more defensible frontier or for repelling the assault of an aggressor is obviously something entirely different from a war fought for the total defeat and unconditional surrender of the enemy. But if the purposes of war may vary, then the measures necessary to achieve these purposes may—indeed must—be equally varied. It can hardly be expected that the principle of humanity will receive the same interpretation in a war fought for essentially unlimited purposes as it will receive in a war waged for distinctly limited ends.

In the final analysis, then, the insistence that even against an aggressor the manner of employing force must remain subject to humanitarian restraints may well prove to be little

---

the "self," it would be difficult to avoid the conclusion that the brief history of this nation's attitude toward the use of nuclear weapons provides one further demonstration of the argument that the potentialities for ethical behavior on the part of collectives remains extremely limited. As long as we retained a monopoly or at least a marked superiority in nuclear weapons and their means of delivery, a policy that sought to reconcile the requirements of a balanced budget with the requirements of the moral law proved relatively easy. That a policy heavily reliant upon the threat of nuclear retaliatory power to deter aggression implied the acceptance, in the event of armed conflict, of a striking disparity between the lives of the enemy we would destroy and the sacrifice of American lives, was simply taken as a matter of fact about which moral qualms seemed irrelevant. Besides, whatever moral doubts that remained over a policy of nuclear deterrence were stilled by the faith placed in the efficacy of the deterrent threat and, if the unexpected nevertheless occurred, in the justice of American purposes in employing force. It is also significant that from the start the effective criticisms directed against deterrence were almost invariably addressed to the purely political and military risks incurred by that policy and not to any alleged moral risks. The increased attention that has been given of late to the latter is obviously not unrelated to the fact of relative nuclear parity between the United States and the Soviet Union; it serves as a reminder that a moral concern over the consequences following from the unrestrained employment of force cannot be divorced from purely prudential considerations whose inspiration is the fear of retaliation in kind.

more than an empty gesture if unrelated to the purposes of war. It is not what the principle of humanity condemns in the abstract, but rather what the principle of military necessity is deemed to permit in the concrete circumstances of war that is decisive. The interpretation of the requirements of humanity will be governed by the interpretation of the requirements of what is militarily necessary.[82] The latter, dependent as they are primarily upon the purposes for which war is fought, may sanction almost any measure and by so doing throw over it the seemingly limitless moral cloak of the principle of humanity.

In this way the use of atomic weapons against Hiroshima and Nagasaki could be and indeed was justified, not only as a military necessity but also as a legitimate application in war of the principle of humanity. There is no reason to question the sincerity of that justification. Given the purposes for which the war against Japan was fought and accepting these purposes as legitimate in themselves, in its context President Truman's statement that "having found the bomb, we have to use it" becomes perfectly clear, both as a judgment of what was militarily necessary and as a claim of what was morally justified.[83] There remains only a small

[82] This point is usually obscured by the insistence with which writers misinterpret the significance of the principles of military necessity and humanity. Thus it is common to read that the principles of military necessity and humanity contradict one another, that they serve opposing purposes, and that the chief task in imposing effective limits on the employment of force requires a realistic balance to be drawn between the requirements of military necessity and considerations of humanity. But the principle of military necessity surely does not allow the employment of force unnecessary or superfluous to the achievement of the purposes of war. Nor does the principle of humanity oppose human suffering or physical destruction as such. It is the unnecessary infliction of human suffering and the wanton destruction of property that is opposed, not only by the principle of humanity but by military necessity as well. But what will prove to be "unnecessary" in this context must largely depend upon the purposes of war.

[83] It has been frequently asserted, however, that even accepting the purposes for which the war against Japan was fought, the use of atomic weapons

step to be taken in order to arrive at a substantially similar justification for using nuclear weapons against the urban centers of an aggressor, should a policy of deterrence fail. Thus a doctrine that begins by insisting upon the continued validity in war of the imperative requirements of humanity ends by justifying in the name of the principle of humanity measures having no discernible limits save those imposed by force itself.

These considerations are no less applicable to the principle distinguishing between the combatant forces and the civilian population of an aggressor state. That distinction, and the

against Hiroshima and Nagasaki was nevertheless unjustified. In all its variations, this argument necessarily depends upon an estimate of the military and political situation existing in the summer of 1945. Its principal contention is that the dropping of the atomic bomb was militarily unnecessary as a measure to exact Japanese surrender. Yet the very nature of the evidence on which this contention must rely made it next to impossible to establish its validity in a conclusive manner at the time. Also it must be noted that the justification for taking a particular measure in war has never depended upon the objective certainty that the measure in question is militarily necessary but only upon the honest conviction at the time of action that the circumstances were such as to render the measure a military necessity. In his well-known account of the decision to use the atomic bomb, Henry Stimson has written: "I felt that to extract a genuine surrender from the Emperor and his military advisers, they must be administered a tremendous shock which would carry convincing proof of our power to destroy the Empire. Such an effective shock would save many times the number of lives, both American and Japanese, that it would cost." "The Decision to Use the Atomic Bomb," Harper's, February, 1947, p. 101. The "facts" upon which Mr. Stimson and others based their judgment may indeed be questioned, as may be the interpretation given those facts. Nevertheless, it is surely hazardous to conclude that in the circumstances and with the information then available, the decision to drop the bomb did not conform to the requirements of military necessity, given the purposes for which the war was fought. Nor can the dropping of the bomb be criticized on moral grounds, if the purpose of unconditional surrender is once sanctioned. Unfortunately, many critics would like to have it both ways: although approving of the purpose for which the war was fought, they nevertheless insist upon condemning a measure judged to be militarily necessary—and in the circumstances not unreasonably so—for achieving this purpose.

consequent obligation to employ force in as discriminating a manner as the necessities of war permit, cannot fail to hold a prominent place in the American doctrine, given its insistence upon clearly separating the evil aggressor and the innocent population. But however sincere and deeply felt the desire to distinguish in war between the guilty few and the innocent many, that desire alone has not prevented and will not prevent the almost complete identification of the two as far as the actual conduct of hostilities is concerned. Sensitive souls may condemn the employment of force in such a manner as to equate an entire population with the actions of a few; they may point to the moral enormity of the methods which result in this equation. Nevertheless, these protestations will carry little weight if they cannot be reconciled (and it is apparent that they cannot be so reconciled) with a war the purposes of which have no clear and readily discernible limits.

Moreover, a sense of guilt about the methods of employing force can always be dampened if not wholly dispelled by an appeal to the military necessities imposed by war. For the principle distinguishing between combatants and noncombatants is governed no less by these necessities than is the principle of humanity. The scope of the immunity granted noncombatants has always depended very largely upon the interpretation given both to the concept of military objective and to the "incidental" injury that may be inflicted upon the noncombatant population in the course of attacking military objectives. The significance of these two criteria will perforce vary as the character of war varies. Here again, it is not what the principle distinguishing combatants from noncombatants forbids in the abstract that is decisive; it is the interpretation military necessity is alleged to impose upon the criteria which determine the significance of this principle in the concrete circumstances of war. With a sufficiently elastic definition of what constitutes a legitimate military objective and a sufficiently broad interpretation of what constitutes permissible "incidental" injury to the civilian population, there is no need ever to deny the continued validity of the principle distinguishing between combatants and noncombatants. In this manner, the World War II bombings of Hiroshima and Nagasaki were justified in that they contained military objectives the destruction of which was alleged to warrant the "incidental" damage done to the civilian population. Little ingenuity is required to carry this reasoning through to its logical extreme, thereby providing a justification for what may amount in practice to the indiscriminate use of nuclear weapons against the urban centers of an aggressor.

II

On the Justice
of Defensive Wars

I

IF THIS NATION'S RESPONSE TO THE PROSPECT OF employing force in the nuclear age has manifested moral complacency, it has also shown a measure of moral anxiety. The principal source of this anxiety must be found in the attempt to reconcile what are conceived to be the requirements of the moral law governing the resort to force with the necessities imposed upon a policy whose aim is to create an international order in which this nation's vital interests may be preserved. Despite the optimistic assumptions informing the American doctrine of the just war—assumptions strongly nourished by a specific historical experience—there is no assurance that such a reconciliation can always be effected. When it cannot, the choice may have to be made either to preserve what are considered to be the nation's vital interests, though at the price of an uneasy conscience, or to retain a good conscience at the risk of sacrificing these interests. Thus, quite apart from the moral implications of the new technology, we would still be confronted with the dilemma of having to choose between resorting to force under ambiguous circumstances or endangering the success of a policy that we have insisted reflects our elementary security interests as a nation.

It is significant that nuclear weapons have not been seen as altering the basic terms of this dilemma. The new technology has not had the effect of changing the central tenet of the American just war doctrine, that the just war is first and foremost the war fought in self or collective defense against armed aggression. Nor have nuclear weapons substantially modified the complacent conviction that the purposes sought in war and the manner of employing force may be derived from and sanctioned by the circumstances in which war is initiated. To be sure, the potentialities of nuclear war have given rise to a heightened sense of moral anxiety over the prospect of employing force. But the principal effect of that anxiety has been to confirm beyond doubt the conviction that force must be banished as an instrument of national policy and that no circumstances can possibly serve to justify the "aggressive" resort to force. The new technology has therefore deepened and strengthened traditional moral convictions by appearing to provide these convictions with a dramatic and seemingly conclusive validation. Rather than providing a novel source of anxiety, nuclear weapons have served primarily to aggravate a traditional dilemma.

Nevertheless, the consequences which presently threaten to attend the use of force cannot but create novel moral dilemmas for a nation which professes to see in its behavior the expression of a liberal-humanitarian ethic. Such a nation is strongly compelled to justify the use of force by pleading at least an approximate coincidence between the protection of the distinctive interests of the nation—for example, its security and continued independence—and the preservation or advancement of values—such as freedom—which cannot be equated simply with distinctively "national" interests.[1] That

[1] Even when the nation's employment of force is seen primarily in terms of an instinctive will to survive, the survival of the nation is still justified by equating it with what are alleged to be transcendent values. Thus a recent statement of American foreign policy declares that the "American objective includes the basic, fundamental one of national survival. A nation, like an individual, need perhaps give no reason for wanting to survive. A deep instinct and an unreasoning will are, in the last analysis, what count. But the age in which we live justifies making this objective explicit and

coincidence has never been easy to establish, if only for the reason that when any nation resorts to force it most obviously does so to protect those interests which are unique to the nation.[2] Nor have men ever possessed a moral calculus enabling them to determine with assurance the circumstances in which the resort to war might find a clear justification in terms of preserving values whose relevance transcends the national community. Even with the noblest of intentions and the most favorable of circumstances, the

affirming it solemnly. . . . Putting the issue in terms of survival confronts foreign policy with its grimmest decision: the resort to force and the possible use of weapons dangerous to civilization itself. It confronts the citizens and their leaders with the ultimate question: upon what grounds do they deem their survival as a nation a good for the sake of which such grave perils must be faced? For Americans, the answer must be that, despite shortcomings and defects, they conceive the United States as standing for enduring values deeply rooted in the aspirations of man." Rockefeller Brothers Fund Special Studies Report, *The Mid-Century Challenge to U. S. Foreign Policy* (1959), pp. 10-11.

[2] ". . . the fact is that every nation is caught in the moral paradox of refusing to go to war unless it can be proved that the national interest is imperiled, and of continuing in the war only by proving that something much more than national interest is at stake. Our nation is not the only community of mankind which is tempted to hypocrisy. Every nation must come to terms with the fact that, though the force of collective self-interest is so great, that national policy must be based upon it; yet also the sensitive conscience recognizes that the moral obligation of the individual transcends his particular community. Loyalty to the community is therefore morally tolerable only if it includes values wider than those of the community." Reinhold Niebuhr, *The Irony of American History* (1952), pp. 36-37. Nevertheless, the claim that in resorting to war the nation thereby preserves values which transcend the national community cannot be dismissed either because the nation has resorted to war primarily to protect its distinctive interests or because the nation never represents these broader values as faithfully as it will invariably pretend. But it may be refuted by a nation's insistence upon resorting to force even though there is a strong probability that in the circumstances the employment of force will prove more destructive of these broader values than would be the case if the nation instead accepted some sacrifice of its interests. Nations have always been notoriously loathe to admit the bare possibility that in employing force such a situation may arise and in this respect America affords no exception.

possibility cannot be precluded that the consequences of using force may prove more destructive to values shared by a civilization or even by the world at large than if the nation, instead, accepts some sacrifice of its interests. Still, this possibility has never appeared in the imposing form it does today. If the equation traditionally drawn between the interests to be protected through force and the moral hazards incurred as a consequence of employing force has always appeared tenuous, this equation has never appeared so tenuous as at present. Indeed, the implications of the new technology for a moral appraisal of force are such as to render all comparisons with past experience of marginal relevance.

Hence, the assertion that the prospect of employing force has always given rise to moral dilemmas is quite true. Nevertheless, the nature and urgency of these dilemmas and the degree to which they permit a satisfactory solution must depend upon the circumstances attending and the consequences following from the employment of force. Nor is it particularly useful to continue to assert that the validity of moral principles governing the employment of force must remain unaffected by the changing conditions and consequences of warfare. Assuming a general consensus on the validity of these principles, the decisive problem of agreeing upon their application in radically changed circumstances would still remain. Save for the fanatic, these changed circumstances must provide the principal difficulty and cause for uncertainty in any moral appraisal of the use of force. The same moral principles that may in one period justify the employment of force in order to defend certain national interests may in another period condemn the resort to war for the protection of these interests. In one period the task of balancing the values to be preserved by the resort to war against the values destroyed through war may create no serious moral problem. In another period—and it is clear that we are in such a period—a growing disproportion between the values to be protected by employing force and the moral hazards incurred if force is once undertaken cannot fail to create seemingly intractible moral dilemmas.

It may well be that it has simply become impossible in the present circumstances to achieve even a reasonably satisfactory compromise between the requirements of political success, as defined primarily in terms of the security and power of the nation, and the requirements of a liberal-humanitarian ethic. At best, that compromise has never been easy to achieve; to the degree that it has been attained, its achievement has been very largely the result of favorable though fortuitous circumstances. It is understandable that this reconciliation of success with the imperatives of the moral law should be ascribed to some unique virtue and that a nation should be reluctant to admit that its past behavior was largely a matter of good fortune. Nevertheless, the moral novelty of the present situation cannot seriously be doubted. On the one hand, the ambiguity of the circumstances in which a successful policy may require the employment of force has no meaningful parallel in the past nor perhaps any clear sanction in doctrine. On the other hand, the protection of legitimate security interests in the least ambiguous of circumstances may well be undertaken only at the risk of sacrificing values that will place the resort to force in grave moral question.

Given the American response to the prospect of employing force, it is understandable that the temptation will arise not only to interpret ambiguous threats to the nation's security as constituting armed aggression but also to interpret threats of varying magnitude to the security interests of the nation as raising the bare issue of national survival. The equation of ambiguous threats with armed aggression is the response of a doctrine which asserts that force need not be employed and therefore ought not to be employed save as a measure of defense against the aggressive use of armed force. The innocence of this equation obviously provides no guarantee that an excessive moral anxiety will not thereby be transformed into an equally excessive moral complacency which pretends that the moral dilemmas attending the employment of force have been finally resolved. To be sure, that complacency must still come to terms with the consequences threatening to follow a war fought with nuclear weapons. Hence, it is not for nothing that threats of varying magnitude are readily assimilated to the issue of national survival itself. For it is only in this manner that the consequences of nuclear war can find an apparent justification. Yet even when the plea of national survival may not prove spurious, there remains the task of demonstrating that the moral law permits the possible destruction of a vast portion of humanity in order to insure the survival of the nation. A persuasive demonstration to this effect has still to be made.

Nor can this issue be turned aside by insisting that nations will in fact take any action considered necessary to preserve their integrity and continued political independence. Even if true, it does not resolve the distinctly moral problem, the problem of providing the justification for such action. And the novelty of this problem stems quite simply from the consideration that although the moral law has always been conceived as sanctioning force for defensive purposes it has never been interpreted as permitting what may well prove to be universal destruction. Thus in a perceptive essay on the theorists of the Anglo-American tradition in foreign affairs, Arnold Wolfers has pointed out that "it was never suggested that national self-preservation itself should be sacrificed to moral principle. Instead, statesmen were urged to combine two basic goals: one, the primary though prudently conceived objective of self-preservation—call it the vital national security interest—the other, implied in such prudence, a fulfillment of the moral law to the maximum compatible with the primary duty of defense." [3] Whether, and to what extent, these two goals will prove compatible, however, must depend upon circumstances, and particularly upon the changing nature of warfare. Given the nature and purposes of war in an earlier period, the assumption of compatibility was not an unreasonable one. But is it possible to reconcile these two goals in the nuclear age? If the "primary duty of defense" results in the destruction of a major part of the world, may this nevertheless be seriously considered a reasonable fulfillment of the moral law? It is one thing to endorse and to act upon the position that the justification for employing force must ultimately rest upon the "higher purposes" of national security and power, and that before these purposes all other considerations may be and ought to be subordinated. It is quite another thing to justify the use of force by pleading a necessary coincidence between these standards and the preservation of values which cannot be equated simply with the security and power of the nation. That coincidence may still occur. To insist that in the nuclear age it must occur is clearly to substitute an ideology in place of the admittedly tragic realities of contemporary world politics.

If the contemporary response this nation has made to the prospect of employing force has manifested a measure of moral uncertainty and unease, that fact alone can hardly occasion surprise or give rise to criticism. On the contrary, what must prove astonishing and invite criticism is how little anxiety has been provoked by this prospect. Moreover, the anxiety that has been apparent has stemmed largely from considerations which not only appear rather irrelevant to the substantive moral issues involved but which frequently seem to obscure these issues. And when this nation's response to the prospect of employing force has not given rise to a conscience uneasy for irrelevant and obscure reasons, it has

[3] Arnold Wolfers and Laurence W. Martin, *The Anglo-American Tradition in Foreign Affairs* (1956), p. xxvii.

all too frequently reflected the complacent belief that the moral dilemmas attending the employment of force may be clearly resolved and that political success may be easily equated with moral achievement.

In view of the traditional American commitment this reluctance to acknowledge moral dilemmas imposed by the new technology may seem anomalous. Yet if the American attitude assumes both the autonomy and the relevance of the moral law for statecraft and consequently presupposes a disparity between successful political action—as defined primarily in terms of the security and power of the nation— and moral action, it ought not to be forgotten that this disparity is nevertheless regarded as no more than temporary. Moral standards may not be considered as inhering in political reality and the requirements of moral action may not be drawn from the requirements of successful action, but this is not interpreted as an admission that there may be a lasting derangement between the two. Instead, it is assumed that "if only the long view of things is taken," the harmony of moral action and successful action is always and necessarily guaranteed. In the American view, therefore, the pursuit of disinterested moral principle turns out to be no more than the pursuit of enlightened self-interest. What may seem in the short run to be political failure appears in the long run to contribute to the security and power of the nation. Hence the harmony between political success and moral achievement remains, although the order in which it is to be achieved is reversed. In the end, there is no divergence found between the imperatives of the moral law and the requirements of effective policy. Moral dilemmas, therefore, are at worst only "provisional," as is the unease that reflects these dilemmas.

These summary remarks may find their most instructive illustration in an inquiry into the contrast drawn by American doctrine between "preventive" and "defensive" wars.

II

Whatever the uncertainties that mark contemporary American policy, at least the dominant attitude maintained with respect to the issue of preventive war appears free from any ambiguity. Since the outset of Soviet-American rivalry, when the issue of preventive war arose, the occasional proposals that this nation might well consider such a policy have unfailingly provoked an indignant response. A policy of preventive war, the prevailing official and private sentiment has insisted, scarcely bears discussion, since from every point of view it must be seen as immoral and wicked. It is repugnant if only for the reason that it implies the false notion of war's inevitability and is therefore an ignominious surrender to irresponsibility. Even more, a policy of preventive war must accept the principle that a means inherently evil may nevertheless be justified in order to achieve what are conceived to be desirable ends. But once this immoral principle is accepted the way is opened for the justification of any crime. Finally, preventive war almost invariably invokes a picture of incredible destruction and chaos, since it is equated with an all-out conflict. Given this identification of preventive war with unlimited conflict, the conclusion seems unavoidable: if preventive war is immoral in any era, it must prove particularly evil at the present juncture.[4]

All of the above points are by now quite familiar, at least in outline. They have been repeated on numerous occasions and have long been accepted almost as a matter of course. Yet these arguments are not self-evident, despite the habit of so regarding them. Nor are they purely moral arguments,

---

[4] See pp. 14-18 for a review of the official response to the issue of preventive war. The views of private individuals and groups have for the most part corresponded very closely to the official view.

although they are usually presented as such. Each depends for its persuasiveness upon assumptions whose validity can scarcely be regarded as beyond dispute. It is, for example, not obvious and has never been obvious why preventive war must be "by definition" an all-out war with no restrictions placed on the manner of employing force.[5] Certainly the bare frequency with which this contention has been advanced cannot be taken as a conclusive test of its validity. Of course, any resort to war in the present circumstances, particularly if involving nuclear Powers directly or even indirectly, may eventuate in an unrestricted war in which nuclear weapons are used indiscriminately. Evidently, a policy of preventive war may also lead to this result. Nevertheless the argument that force must of necessity be equated with total and indiscriminate force is not self-evident and even the new technology does not give this argument a compelling quality.

[5] In his impressive study of strategy in the nuclear age, Bernard Brodie uses the term "preventive war" "to describe a premeditated attack by one country against another, which is unprovoked in the sense that it does not wait upon a specific aggression or other overt action by the target state, and in which the chief and most immediate objective is the destruction of the latter's over-all military power and especially its strategic air power." *Strategy in the Missile Age* (1959), p. 227. Presumably, "aggression" here means "armed aggression" simply in the sense of initiating the use of armed force. Brodie goes on to write: "The phrase 'preventive war' implies inevitably the unprovoked slaughter of millions of persons, mostly innocent of responsibility, on the inherently unprovable assumption that our safety requires it" (pp. 236-37). But preventive war does not "inevitably" imply this unless we first define preventive war to imply what Brodie insists it must inevitably imply. Of course, once preventive war is so defined then it is simply redundant to insist that preventive war "implies inevitably" those consequences which "by definition" we have already assigned to it. This is an example of what may be called the "self-fulfilling definition." Besides, is the "innocence" of the millions slaughtered in a preventive war a reason for condemning *only* preventive war? Are these millions any less innocent in a "defensive" war, which is nevertheless characterized by the same measures that "by definition" must presumably mark a preventive war? Or is the moral question raised by the employment of incredibly destructive weapons to turn upon what our safety requires or is thought to require rather than upon the innocence of the slaughtered millions?

Nor is it obvious that preventive war presupposes in any literal sense the idea of war's inevitability and is therefore a surrender to irresponsibility. The ideas that may inform a policy of preventive war need not assume the notion of war's inevitability. The "necessity" alleged to inhere in the advocacy of preventive war is, in fact, thoroughly compatible with the view that nations need never employ force, whether "aggressively" or "defensively," so long as they are prepared to accept the consequences of their renunciation.[6] It is not obvious, however, that nations need never employ force, again whether "aggressively" or "defensively," even though they may wish to preserve what they conceive to be their vital interests. If there are very few unambiguous lessons to be learned from history, this is surely not one of them. And whatever the merits of the interpretation we have given

[6] See, for example, the 1950 report of the Commission appointed by the Federal Council of Churches, issued under the title "Christian Conscience and Weapons of Mass Destruction," *Christianity and Crisis*, December 11, 1950, p. 166. In rejecting preventive war the Commission declared that: "To accept general war as inevitable is to treat ourselves as helpless objects carried by a fated tide of events rather than as responsible men." This statement is, of course, unexceptionable. It is also somewhat beside the point, however, if the issue of "inevitability" with respect to a policy of preventive war is understood in the relative sense discussed above in the text. And it is difficult to see in what other sense the "inevitability" of preventive war can be meaningfully considered. The report goes on to conclude that "to accept the inevitability of war is strategically wrong. It is morally wrong because it is a surrender to irresponsibility. It is religiously wrong because it involves a pretension on the part of man to know the future with an assurance not granted to man." Whether preventive war is "strategically wrong" surely cannot be decided in the abstract, but must depend upon the concrete circumstances in which a policy of preventive war is considered. Circumstances may also determine whether preventive war is a "surrender to irresponsibility." To be sure, the Commission's rejection of preventive war also rested on the equation of preventive war with an unlimited conflict involving "consequences which will be horrible according to responsible calculation, and may be more terrible than any calculations." But the rejection of preventive war for this reason raises quite a different argument—one which could well apply to "defensive" wars as well.

to our past experience as a nation, there is no compelling
reason for assuming that this interpretation has the quality
of a universal law.

The objection may still be raised that preventive war
represents a surrender to irresponsibility since it involves
the acceptance of a certain evil in order to avoid what can
only be a less-than-certain danger. Without doubt, preventive war does involve precisely that. But if for this reason
preventive war is taken to represent a surrender to irresponsibility, then any action involving the acceptance of a
certain evil in order to avoid a still greater potential evil
is to be equated with irresponsibility. The acceptance of
this equation of uncertainty and irresponsibility would damn
the most characteristic and certainly the most critical decisions the statesman must make. It is part of the very
essence of these decisions that they will normally be marked
with uncertainty. An insistence upon refusing to accept
what may at the time be a limited evil until the menace of
a potentially far greater evil has become a virtual certainty
may simply mean that action will be taken only when it
is no longer possible either to prevent the greater evil or to
set limits to the consequences which resistance to evil will
entail.[7] Preventive war may indeed represent a surrender

---

[7] Had it been possible in 1936 or 1937 to conduct successfully a preventive
war against Nazi Germany, would this have been a surrender to irresponsibility? Might not the "certain evil" that would have resulted from such
a war have been much less than the evil that resulted from war when it
finally did come? At the outset of the cold war the military expert of the
New York Times, after declaring that preventive war was an "alien and
repugnant concept," solemnly assured his readers that: "If war has to come
it is far better that it come twenty years from now than today." Hanson
Baldwin, "The Price of War," *Harpers,* July, 1948, p. 26. This is not to
suggest that good reasons for rejecting preventive war did not exist in the
earlier period of the cold war. Even with the benefit of hindsight a strong
case for rejection can be made, although one that must now appear far less
persuasive than the arguments urged at the time. The relevant point,
however, is that neither the political nor the moral considerations involved
are as self-evident as American doctrine has insisted.

to irresponsibility in certain and perhaps in most circumstances. In some circumstances, however, it may well be the refusal to undertake a preventive war that will appear as a surrender to irresponsibility. But there is no compelling reason for assuming that this matter can be resolved in the abstract and by an appeal to the assumptions sketched out above.

It is perhaps too much to expect that the reasoning which informs a doctrine so insistent on condemning preventive war will also be applied to the conduct of a "defensive" war. Yet the inconsistency in American doctrine between the attitude held toward preventive war and the view taken with respect to the conduct of a defensive war is extraordinary by any standard. Precisely the reasons used to condemn preventive war become the reasons used to defend the manner and purposes of a defensive war. What was the justification given for waging a defensive war to the end of "unconditional surrender"? Obviously, to prevent the possibility of a revival of aggression. If this purpose necessitated the acceptance of certain evil in terms of the manner of conducting war, which it certainly did, this was never interpreted as a surrender to irresponsibility. On the contrary, it would be irresponsible, so this argument runs, not to extirpate the roots of aggression. If these means impose a certain evil, they are nevertheless justified in order to achieve a desirable end. Is not the same reasoning equally apparent in a policy bent upon deterring aggression by threatening potential aggressors either with utter annihilation or with severe punishment should they once seek to carry out their evil designs? In either case, the deterrent threat must hold out the promise of measures which may not only exceed in their scope the measures of an aggressor but which are designed to achieve a far more ambitious end than merely to repel an aggressor. That end is to prevent further aggression either by annihilating the aggressor or by punishing him with sufficient severity so that he will be neither able nor willing to undertake further aggression. The policy of deterrence has been based throughout on the assumption that should it once prove necessary to employ force in order to resist aggression a certain evil—indeed, a radical evil—may be accepted to achieve a desirable end.

It is also noteworthy that although the above assumptions have almost invariably appeared as inseparable features of arguments condemning preventive war, they nevertheless bear no necessary or logical relationship to one another; they may even be seen as leading to quite disparate moral arguments, depending upon which assumption is accorded principal emphasis. Undoubtedly, the assumption that equates preventive war with all-out conflict provides additional and persuasive support for the conviction that nations need never employ force "aggressively" as an instrument of national policy. Nevertheless, if the condemnation of preventive war is based upon the incredibly destructive character such a war implies, this assumption does not merely make what must presumably be an immoral act in any period and in any circumstances still more heinous in a period of nuclear technology.

The condemnation of preventive war because of what is assumed to be the highly destructive character of such a war necessarily presupposes a view which judges the justice or injustice of war at least as much in terms of the consequences of employing force as it does in terms of other criteria. It does not imply, however, any assumption about the "need" to resort to force as an instrument of national policy. Hence, the preventive and militarily "aggressive" resort to force to protect a vital and legitimate interest of the state is condemned, whatever the necessity of such a measure, because of the consequences expected to follow from the employment of force. But the same conclusion may also be reached with respect to what is militarily a purely "defensive" employment of force. On the other hand, if the condemnation of preventive war rests primarily upon the assumption that such a war is simply unnecessary, the justice or injustice of war will be determined by the act of initiating the use of armed force. The consequences of employing force, whether aggressively or defensively, may of course constitute a subordinate concern. Obviously, they cannot form a central concern since the "necessity" of employing force is not considered here as something proportionate to the consequences expected to follow from the employment of force. For the "necessity" in this instance is not a "moral necessity" but one which purports to inhere in the nature of state relations.

To be sure, a policy of preventive war obviously does imply that certain means, the "aggressive" resort to force, are justified in order to achieve certain ends. But it is absurd to argue that whatever the circumstances the advocacy of preventive war must be regarded as implying acceptance of the principle that in statecraft any means are justified. The insistence that preventive war must accept any means as justified is an illuminating commentary though on the manner in which this nation has conceived of waging a preventive war. It is not so much the act of resorting to force that has in fact provoked the "any means are justified" argument but the willingness to contemplate using "any means" once in war, preventive or otherwise. In a sense, the argument we have used in condemning preventive war may be interpreted as an indirect acknowledgment of the moral hazards arising from the manner in which we have conceived waging a defensive war. Nevertheless, there are preventive wars and preventive wars. The advocacy of preventive war in one set of circumstances does not require the advocacy of preventive war in any and all circumstances. Nor is there any necessary inconsistency of principle involved in advocat-

ing a preventive war in one set of circumstances and condemning the preventive resort to force in another set of
circumstances.

The same interest may even be at issue in both sets of
circumstances, though not only that interest. Even though
the interest may be the same, the consequences following
from the attempt to realize that interest through force may
be profoundly different. Thus, the American interest in a
Soviet withdrawal from Eastern Europe has remained essentially unchanged through the vicissitudes that have marked
the cold war. But the probable consequences of attempting
to realize that interest, if necessary through the preventive
resort to force, have changed and in a radical manner. No
necessary inconsistency of principle is involved if, in order
to realize that interest, the preventive use of force was advocated in one set of circumstances and nevertheless is later
condemned in changed circumstances, though the interest
itself remains unaltered. The reason for this is clear enough.
While our interest in a Soviet withdrawal from Eastern
Europe may remain unchanged, we have and have always
had other interests which may conflict with or be jeopardized
by the measures required to realize this particular interest.
The condemnation of preventive war follows from the
appreciation that in the given circumstances the probable
consequences of resorting to force would be to sacrifice these
other more critical interests.

Besides, the moral complacency with which a disarmingly
simple version of the means-ends argument has been used
to condemn preventive war seems particularly gratuitous in
view of the fact that many of its advocates are not really
entitled to its use. Given a markedly voluntaristic interpretation of international conflict, the conviction readily arises
that nations need not resort to force as an instrument of
national policy in order to protect their legitimate interests.
Preventive war as a means of policy is condemned not be-

cause of an absolute moral principle forbidding these means regardless of circumstances and purposes, but simply because the means are judged to be unnecessary. Thus the means-ends argument that proceeds from the assumption that preventive war is unnecessary must be sharply distinguished from the position that condemns it as a means of policy while nevertheless admitting that circumstances may well arise in which preventive war appears as the only effective method for protecting a nation's interests. The latter position declares, in effect, that however strong the desire to achieve certain ends and despite the legitimacy of these ends, there remains an absolute moral injunction forbidding certain means. It may be that the means, preventive war, are indispensable if the ends sought are to be attained. Even so, the means must be rejected because of their intrinsic immorality, and because they are forbidden in any circumstances. On the other hand, the assumption that preventive war is unnecessary for the protection of a nation's vital interests evidently need not also imply an interpretation of the moral law as requiring the subordination of these interests to an absolute moral principle which forbids certain means. For the need to make such a choice presupposes the possibility of a conflict arising between the necessities of policy and the requirements of the moral law, and that possibility has been precluded. What appears as a sacrifice of interest before the absolute requirements of the moral law turns out to be no sacrifice at all but rather a coincidence of expediency and morality.

III

The American condemnation of preventive war is not to be interpreted as suggesting the conviction that force must always be regarded as an instrument of injustice. The vehemence with which preventive war is condemned has its counterpart in the insistence with which defensive wars are seen as conforming to the dictates of the moral law. It is apparent that the moral assurance marking this absolute repudiation of preventive war must presuppose that a clear and simple distinction can be drawn between a preventive war and a defensive war. This distinction provides the basis for equally clear and simple moral judgments. Yet it is also apparent that if such a distinction is at all possible, it is by insisting that the critical test, and indeed the only relevant test, must consist in the act of initially resorting to armed force. Hence, the causes that have ultimately led to the outbreak of violence, as well as the manner in which and the purposes for which force is employed, must be regarded as irrelevant if the clarity of this distinction is to be preserved. Once the relevance of these latter factors is in principle admitted, a simple distinction may evidently become very complex and an equally simple moral judgment may become subject to endless qualification and consequent uncertainty. A preventive war must signify, therefore, nothing more nor less than the act of initiating armed violence, of striking the first blow, and its condemnation must presumably follow from this fact. Conversely, a defensive war must signify nothing more nor less than the act of responding to the "aggressive" use of force, and the legitimacy of defensive wars presumably follows from this fact.

The clarity and simplicity of the distinction thus drawn between preventive and defensive wars cannot be doubted. If a consistent adherence to this distinction may nevertheless lead to unwanted and even to ludicrous consequences, it is not because of a lack of clarity but because the "logic" of this distinction so obviously violates practical judgments formed from historical experience. To be sure, preventive war necessarily implies the act of initiating armed force and, in this specific sense, is "aggressive." But it does not follow that a preventive war is necessarily aggressive in any other meaningful sense of the term. A preventive war may be undertaken out of defensive considerations and may be fought for defensive purposes. Even though victorious, the state waging a preventive war may abstain from aggrandizement. The state against which a preventive war is undertaken may by its policies have clearly provoked the preventive use of force; those policies though stopping short of the overt use of armed force against the territorial integrity and political independence of other states, may nevertheless have had as their purpose the impairment if not the radical change of the *status quo*. Nor is there anything to prevent a state that has "defensively" responded to the "aggressive" use of force from harboring at the start expansionist or perhaps punitive desires and from seeking to realize those desires should it prove to be victorious in war. A preventive war may be defensive in every sense save for the initially "aggressive" act of resorting to armed force, and the state made the object of the preventive use of force may wage a war that is anything but defensive except for the fact that it did not literally initiate the armed conflict.

These considerations are, or at least should be, commonplaces. Admittedly, they do not resolve the distinctly moral issues raised by the preventive use of force, and there is no suggestion here that they do. Despite their admission the moral judgment may nevertheless be made that preventive war, regardless of the precise form it may take, is to be condemned and that if this rejection of preventive war may indeed give rise to injustice, the continued acceptance of the principle that nations may resort in certain circumstances to the preventive use of force will work still greater evil. But whatever the merits of this position it is necessary to insist that they do not stem from the simple distinction between preventive and defensive wars noted above; nor do they validate the assumption that this simple distinction of itself provides the basis for equally simple moral judgments. Nevertheless, the traditional justification for preventive war stemmed from these considerations.

"Wars preventive upon just fears are true defensives, as well as upon actual invasions," Francis Bacon observed four centuries ago in summarizing this traditional justification.[8] Given a society that has yet to achieve an order which can effectively provide a reasonable measure of security for its component parts, the preventive use of force "upon just fears" of attack may not only be prudential behavior but may also constitute no more than the exercise of self-defense. The same reasoning, when applied to the international society as a whole rather than to the individual state, served to justify preventive war as a means to the end of maintaining a semblance of order based upon a balance of power. It is almost a truism by now to state that war, including preventive war, was not conceived to be inconsistent with a system of international order founded upon the principle of a balance of power. But if the balance of power is conceived to be a just principle of order, whatever its inadequacies when compared with the order enjoyed by domestic

[8] Francis Bacon, "Considerations Touching a War with Spain," cited in Wolfers and Martin, *The Anglo-American Tradition in Foreign Affairs,* p. 14. The theme of preventive war has always been one of the most persistent in Western moral and political thought. Yet whether for a Thucydides in his *History of the Peloponnesian War* or for a John Stuart Mill in his essay "A Few Words on Non-Intervention," the justification of preventive war "upon just fears" of attack is accepted in principle. There are, of course, exceptions—or seeming exceptions. There is Grotius' counsel to rely upon "Divine Providence, and on a wariness free from reproach" rather than upon force for "protection against uncertain fears." But even Grotius does not condemn the preventive use of force where the power and *animus* of the potential adversary amounts to "moral certainty"—a term conveniently left undefined. See H. Lauterpacht, "The Grotian Tradition in International Law," *The British Yearbook of International Law,* XXIII (1946), 35-39. And for a recent and perceptive analysis of the recurring issue of preventive war in a system of independent states, see Kenneth N. Waltz, *Man, the State and War* (1959), pp. 198-238.

societies, then war undertaken to preserve an equilibrium of power must also be considered as a just use of force. The classic doctrines of the balance of power therefore presupposed both the necessity and the legitimacy of preventive war as a means, though an extreme means, for preserving an international equilibrium. So also did doctrines of international law prevalent in the eighteenth and nineteenth centuries seek to justify preventive wars undertaken to maintain or restore the balance of power which was looked upon as essential for the continued effectiveness of international law.[9]

The traditional justification given for preventive war was, of course, always marked by ambiguities and internal contradictions, which made it a ready instrument for aggressive and expansionist policies and a convenient receptacle into which the most varied national interests could be poured. What precise circumstances would constitute a just fear of attack permitting preventive action, and who would determine when these circumstances were present as well as when they had ceased to obtain? If traditional doctrine left the former question conveniently obscure by invoking the formulas of "vital interests" and "self-preservation," it answered the latter question in circular fashion. The state taking preventive action might arrogate to itself the right to determine the presence of those largely undefined circumstances in which force was alleged to represent no more than the exercise of self-defense. Other states might also claim a right to challenge the legitimacy of preventive measures, particularly when such measures threatened or were alleged

[9] "Under certain circumstances and conditions, many political causes of war may correctly be called just causes. Only such individuals as lack insight into history and human nature can, for instance, defend the opinion that a war is unjust which has been caused . . . by the desire to maintain the balance of power, which under the present conditions and circumstances is the basis of international law." L. Oppenheim, *International Law* (1921), II, 81. Oppenheim's view was a lingering echo of a position widespread among earlier writers.

to threaten the international equilibrium. But this possibility obviously could not resolve the question at issue; it could merely raise it anew. If there is no guarantee against the misuse which a state may make of its "right" to determine the circumstances in which the preventive use of force is justified, there is also no guarantee that the challenge to this interpretation will somehow reflect a truer conception of legitimate defensive measures.

Nor are the requirements of "legitimate defense," when considered from the standpoint of the interests of a particular nation, necessarily identical with the requirements of an international order dependent upon the effective maintenance of a balance of power. To the degree that the traditional justification for preventive war sought to encompass both the legitimate defensive interests of the nation and the interest in maintaining an international equilibrium of power, it could do so only by assuming that the two coincided and that the preventive use of force for maintaining the balance would not conflict with the interests of nations in preserving their security and independence. This assumption cannot be dismissed simply as a transparent ideology intended to provide a spurious justification for expansionist policies by the device of appealing to the broader community interest in order. However misused by states, the assumption was substantially valid. Yet it is clear that the requirements of an international order based upon a balance of power might, and indeed did, require the sacrifice of what were otherwise conceived as the legitimate defensive interests of the individual nation. Although the justification of the balance of power ultimately lay in its promise to bring both order and security to the nations which made up the international society, the price of order might nevertheless require the sacrifice of a particular nation's security and perhaps even of its independence. Obscured by doctrine, this paradox has always inhered in the operation of the balance of power and, consequently, in one of the characteristic methods of balance-of-power policies, preventive war. If the latter was nevertheless justified as sanctioning the use of force only for defensive purposes, the question always remained: defensive for whom? In practice the answer could seldom be in doubt, given the disparity in power that has always existed among nations.[10]

Even more tenuous, however, was the attempt to reconcile the traditional justification given for preventive war with what purported to be a system of law. If international law depended for its effectiveness upon the maintenance of a balance of power, this legal system had somehow to accommodate itself to the employment of methods which not only escaped legal control but which seemed almost to deny the very possibility of a legal ordering of state relations. War—preventive war included—was at once the indispensable prerequisite for and the insurmountable obstacle to the realization of an effective legal order. Hence, the apparent anomaly arose of a legal system which did not, and seemingly could not, consistently draw the most elementary distinction that any system of law must make, the distinction between the lawful and the unlawful use of force.[11]

[10] It is an illusion, however, to believe that this particular criticism applies only to the traditional balance of power system. As will presently be seen, it applies with equal force to the system of international order initially envisaged in the Charter of the United Nations. Indeed, in this respect, the chief difference between the traditional balance of power system and the system of the Charter is that the latter sought to make explicit and to legitimize what the former left obscure and never quite dared to legitimize. Erich Hula's observation that the rules of the Charter relating to enforcement may be considered "a mere legalization and formalization of the diplomatic conceptions and procedures characteristic of the concert system of collective intervention practiced by the European Pentarchy in the nineteenth century" is, if anything, a restrained judgment. See Erich Hula, "The Evolution of Collective Security" in Arnold Wolfers, ed., *Alliance Policy in the Cold War* (1959), p. 87.

[11] To be sure, the traditional system did draw a distinction of sorts between the lawful and unlawful use of force by nations in time of peace.

According to the prevailing legal doctrine of the nineteenth century the act of resorting to war was neither legal nor illegal, but "extralegal" in the sense of an event occurring in nature, for example, an earthquake or flood. However fictitious this doctrine, it nevertheless accurately reflected the dilemma of an order dependent for its effectiveness upon the maintenance of a balance of power, and consequently upon methods which remained impervious to effective legal control. The principal function of international law was the delimitation of the various states' respective spheres of competence and the protection of their legitimate interests. Yet the customary liberty accorded to states to resort to war in effect denied this function by permitting one state to deprive another state through war of its most fundamental rights, including the right of existence itself. In these circumstances, whatever virtue this earlier system of international law possessed rested upon a principle of order which, paradoxically enough, also proved to be the system's greatest vice. To the extent that this apparent contradiction was resolved, it was not on the level of law. Instead, one must look to the political and moral inhibitions that operated to restrain balance-of-power policies in preceding centuries.[12]

Thus the rule forbidding intervention by one state in the affairs of another state and the rules governing the right to take forceful acts of reprisal testify to this distinction. Nevertheless, the value of this distinction was bound to prove limited since a state had only to consider acts of force directed against it, however legitimate those acts may have been, as acts of war in order to regain a complete liberty of action.

[12] Hans Morgenthau rightly points out: "Of the temperateness and indecisiveness of the political contests, from 1648 to the Napoleonic Wars and then again from 1815 to 1914, the balance of power is not only the cause but also the metaphorical and symbolic expression as well as the technique of realization. Before the balance of power could impose its restraints upon the power aspirations of nations through the mechanical interplay of opposing forces, the competing nations had first to restrain themselves by accepting the system of the balance of power as the common framework of their endeavors." *Politics Among Nations* (2nd ed., 1954), p. 199.

If the ambiguities always inherent in the traditional justification of preventive war admittedly made it a ready instrument of state interest, do similar ambiguities mark contemporary justifications of force? Does the criticism that has served to discredit this traditional doctrine also provide a significant commentary on modern notions of legitimate self-defense? These questions must inevitably arise, if only for the reason that apart from the most restrictive interpretation of the right of self-defense, the legitimacy of the preventive use of force is not precluded in contemporary doctrines of self-defense. Even more, the justification given for taking "anticipatory" measures of a defensive nature continues to rest largely upon an acceptance of the essential principle which formed the basis of the traditional justification of preventive war. The frequency with which preventive war may be placed in contrast with a war of self-defense cannot obscure the fact that if the "anticipatory" use of force remains as an integral feature of the right of self-defense the legitimacy of preventive war is preserved.

Indeed, it is instructive and certainly far more meaningful to look upon doctrines of self-defense prevalent in recent decades as attempts to purify the traditional justification of preventive war rather than as efforts to reject that justification entirely. It is characteristic of these attempts that they have sought to "de-politicize" traditional doctrine, presumably by cleansing it of its dangerous features and thereby rendering it compatible with an international system in which the resort to force as an instrument of national policy is forbidden. They have accordingly assumed a predominantly legal expression. Whereas in the old system the "right" of the nation to employ force defensively remained at best only a vague principle of political morality subject to endless abuse, in the new order the defensive employment of force has become an allegedly clear principle of legal right. Presumably the vice of traditional doctrine was the practically

limitless discretion it gave to states. The virtue attributed
to contemporary doctrines is that they have placed substantive restrictions on the employment of force and have
at last made possible the drawing of a meaningful distinction
between the illegitimate use of force by a nation and its
legitimate exercise in self-defense.

Yet these claims have never been persuasively demonstrated.[13] Instead, what have been apparent are the ambiguities marking attempts to apply by analogy to the
international society a principle drawn from the domestic
order of the state. Contemporary doctrines of self-defense
necessarily presuppose the possibility of drawing a meaningful parallel between the application of self-defense to the
relations among individuals within the state and the application of this principle to the relations among nations. The
artificial character of the parallel is no less striking than
the fallacies on which it rests. Within the highly centralized
order of the state the principle of self-defense plays a limited
and subordinate role. The right or privilege of the individual to employ force in self-defense is a severely controlled
exception to the monopoly of force held by the state. Its purpose is to enable the individual to avoid a specific evil in
the form of violence or the immediate threat of violence.
The strictly preventive function of self-defense does not
confer upon the individual a right to ensure order or to
obtain justice, for these functions are reserved to the state.
Self-defense here has neither a repressive nor a punitive
function. Finally, the apparent right of self-judgment that
forms a concomitant of the act of self-defense is only provisional and always subject to later investigation and adjudication; the strict control exercised by the state over the
operation of self-defense is clear.

[13] One of the best surveys of the problems raised by contemporary
doctrines of self-defense remains the essay of Émile Giraud, "La Théorie
de la Légitime Défense," *Recueil des Cours*, XLIX (1934-III), 691-865.

The transformation that occurs when the principle of self-defense is applied to the behavior of collective political entities is not merely of a quantitative but of a qualitative character. Within the state self-defense is a principle of order only in a special and closely restricted sense; when applied to the greater society of nations it is far from constituting a subordinate principle of order. Indeed, to the extent that the former freedom of states to employ force becomes progressively restricted, self-defense must increasingly become not simply an important principle but the critical principle of international order. This result obviously contradicts the experience attending the development of the state. Yet it is rendered inevitable if the progressive restrictions placed on the employment of force are not accompanied by parallel change in the structural features of the international society. Force may be in principle forbidden to states as an instrument of national policy. At the same time, no viable alternative to the age-old institution of self-redress may emerge. In these circumstances, the scope of the right of self-defense must very largely determine the meaning of security, since a right of self-redress that nevertheless forbids the threat or use of force may always prove insufficient to the task of achieving security and thereby be deprived of any real utility.

Given this near equation of security and self-defense the tendency to expand the limits of self-defense—or to leave those limits very vague—is almost inevitable. The right of self-defense is applied not only to the state's "physical person," its territorial integrity, but also to those interests which collectively comprise the nation's security and consequently its "existence" in the broader sense of political independence. For this reason alone, extended interpretations of self-defense cannot evoke a meaningful analogy between the individual's right to defend his physical person against unlawful acts of violence and the nation's right to protect its "physical person," its territorial integrity, against similar acts. That analogy is itself difficult enough to sustain, depending as it must upon the assumption that the "physical" defense of the collective poses no problems— political or moral—essentially different from the physical defense of the individual. If an analogy is to be drawn in the case of extended interpretations of self-defense, however, it must be between the individual's right to defend his person against violent attack and the state's right to protect those legitimate interests which collectively comprise its security, and consequently its "existence" in the broader sense, against injurious action, violent or otherwise.

Since uncertainty has always prevailed with respect to the scope and meaning of the right of political independence, an equal uncertainty has prevailed with respect to the scope of the right of self-defense. Nor is this uncertainty dispelled by the assertion that the right of political independence may be defined in terms of the correlative duty of non-intervention. Even if it is assumed that the duty of non-intervention provides sufficient guarantee of the right of independence, no clear agreement exists or has ever existed on the scope of the duty of nonintervention. It is clear that not all forcible interference in the domestic or foreign affairs of another state can be regarded as illegitimate acts of inter-vention. In particular, measures of self-defense taken by a state may represent forcible interference in the affairs of the state against which these measures are directed, though they are nevertheless legitimate. But if the scope of the duty of nonintervention is largely dependent upon the determination of the right of self-defense, one uncertainty is made dependent for its clarification upon yet another uncertainty. To assert that the content of the right of political independence may be found in the correlative duty of nonintervention is simply to shift the problem, not to resolve it.

There is, of course, the further consideration that a state's independence may be impaired by the behavior of another state, although the latter does not employ force nor perhaps even the threat of force. To the extent that intervention is held to encompass only those acts of interference in the affairs of another state that take an imperative or dictatorial form and involve force or the threat of force, the duty of nonintervention becomes irrelevant in dealing with behavior that may just as effectively jeopardize political independence. It may even be that behavior threatening a state's security and independence is not forbidden at all by international law. Indeed, many of the more novel methods of impairing a state's independence through so-called "indirect aggression" remain on the periphery of law, and some appear to escape legal regulation altogether. It is therefore argued that a right of political independence may be deprived of any real meaning if it does not permit states to take, if necessary, forceful measures of self-defense against such methods. Yet it is equally true that a steady expansion of the acts in response to which states may employ force, on the plea that independence requires the resort to force, may easily deprive a right of self-defense of any real meaning.

If the substantive rights on behalf of which force may be employed remain both expansive and ill-defined, if all that can be said with assurance is that in some vague manner these rights encompass the "existence" of the state, how does this constitute an improvement over the now discredited traditional doctrine? If it is no less difficult to define the "rights" essential to a nation's security than it is to define the "vital interests" of a nation, can a meaningful distinction be drawn between a principle of political morality which establishes "vital interests" as the criterion for the resort to force and a principle of law which requires that force used in self-defense must follow the violation or threatened violation of "rights"? That a right to the preventive use of force has been transformed from a principle of political morality into a principle of law is surely no necessary sign of progress if the ambiguities that marked the former principle continue to mark the latter principle as well. The plea of "vital interests" as a justification for employing force may no longer be permitted. Still, it is not easy to see what other significance this change has as long as the "rights" states may still protect by force, if necessary, are not rigidly circumscribed. Whereas in the traditional justification for preventive war the plea of vital interests was plainly acknowledged, in contemporary doctrines of self-defense the formal rejection of this plea requires that it make its reappearance in the guise of legal rights rather than of "mere political interest." It is not for this reason any less important.[14]

To be sure, there remain other restraints that must presumably govern the exercise of legitimate self-defense. Thus the danger that gives rise to the right to employ force in self-defense must be immediate and overwhelming and leave no possibility for recourse to alternative means of protection. In addition, the use of force in self-defense must always

[14] These remarks find their most obvious and instructive illustration in the perennial dispute over whether and how to define aggression. Presumably, the significance of defining aggression is that the concept, once defined, would provide the basis for the legitimate employment of force, whether by a security organization in the form of "sanctions" or by nations in the form of measures of self or collective defense. In large measure, then, the problem of defining aggression appears as the reverse of the problem of defining self-defense. Consequently, the insistence that aggression cannot be defined, that it is impossible to encompass its meaning within the terms of a formal definition, amounts to an insistence that self-defense cannot be defined. At first consideration, it may appear inexplicable that an insistence upon the undesirability, or even the impossibility, of defining aggression has gone hand in hand with an insistence that the "notion" of aggression is nevertheless of critical importance for the task of securing international order and justice. But what may appear inexplicable at first consideration becomes perfectly clear once it is understood that aggression is to each nation roughly identical with those acts of other nations which, taken collectively, may threaten what each nation conceives to be its "vital interests."

prove reasonable, and it may prove reasonable only if it is proportionate to the end of protecting those interests that are endangered. Any use of force in excess of this purpose is forbidden, since action taken in self-defense should have a strictly preventive character.[15]

Obviously, none of these requirements can be expected to prove self-evident in its application. Given the circumstances that normally mark the exercise of self-defense among nations, or rather the claims to the exercise of self-defense, each requirement must raise questions necessarily dependent upon complex political and military considerations. The immediacy of the danger to the security of a state need not, and indeed cannot be gauged simply in terms of overt action of an injurious nature; it is precisely the purpose of self-defense to prevent, if possible, the commission of such injurious action. Inevitably, the danger held to justify the taking of preventive measures in self-defense will depend upon an interpretation of the significance of behavior that falls short of being overt and consequently unambiguous. Even more, if the uncertainty to be tolerated before resorting to preventive measures of force must be related to the nature of the danger posed, the nature of the danger will depend not only upon the *animus* thus far manifested by the other party, but also upon the means of injury the other party has at its disposal. Hence, the nature and immediacy of the danger that may serve to justify preventive war as a measure of legitimate self-defense cannot reasonably be

[15] A recent study of the right of self-defense in international law concludes that: "The nature of the measures taken under the privilege of self-defense vary according to the form which the danger takes, and the criterion of the legality of the measures taken in self-defense is proportionality. The measures taken must be in proportion to the danger and must never be excessive or go beyond what is strictly required for the protection of the substantive rights which are endangered. This view . . . rejects any artificial distinction between measures involving the use of force and those not involving the use of force." D. W. Bowett, *Self-Defense in International Law* (1958), pp. 269-70.

divorced from the technology of war. Changes in the latter cannot but affect the manner in which the requirements of self-defense are applied. A danger sufficiently immediate and overwhelming to warrant the recourse to preventive measures is evidently then something quite different in the present period of nuclear-missile weapons from what it was in the period that preceded the new technology.

No doubt, it is quite true that in any period certain behavior will clearly prove less ambiguous than other behavior in the threat it poses to a nation's security, and that despite the ambiguities characterizing relations among nations in an age of subversion on the one extreme and nuclear-missile attack on the other extreme there still remain situations permitting very little uncertainty as to their ultimate significance. But it is precisely the marginal situation that must provide the critical test of the claims made on behalf of contemporary doctrines of self-defense. For the really clear cases of self-defense may prove to be the fatal cases as well. The purpose of self-defense, however, is presumably to enable nations to protect their essential rights and not to insure that their epitaph will testify to their lawful behavior.

The uncertainties inherent in the applications of these requirements of self-defense to the conduct of nations also present ample opportunities to clothe aggressive behavior in the guise of defensive action. It is particularly the requirement of "proportionality" that gives rise to such opportunities. In its abstract formulation this requirement declares that acts taken in self-defense may not be disproportionate to the danger threatened, and that they will prove disproportionate if they exceed in manner or in purpose the necessity provoking them.[16] Does this merely mean that

---

[16] A distinction must be drawn between the requirement of proportionality in contemporary legal doctrines of self-defense and the requirement of proportionality in the classic *bellum justum* doctrine. The latter requires

acts taken in self-defense must be strictly limited to *repelling* the immediate danger and no more? Or does the requirement of proportionality imply that action in self-defense may be directed to *removing* the danger, on the ground that a right of self-defense is without substance if it does not permit removal of the danger which initially justified the resort to self-defense?[17] If the former interpretation is accepted, difficulties will still remain in placing meaningful limitations on the exercise of self-defense.[18] But these difficulties may prove relatively insignificant by comparison with those emerging from the latter interpretation. When has the danger that justified the resort to force in self-defense been removed? An attack may be repelled, or a threatened attack may be prevented, but the danger may persist. The state that contends it is acting only in self-defense may nevertheless insist that the danger has not passed so long as those circumstances persist which gave rise to the exercise of self-defense. If this reasoning is once accepted, what are the practical limits to the exercise of self-defense? The state acting "defensively" may plausibly contend that the danger

that the evil imposed by war be outweighed by the good sought on the part of those who have a just cause and are inspired by the "right intent," the intent to maintain justice in the interest of the common good. In a recent restatement of this requirement Father Murray declares that "consideration must be given to the proportion between the damage suffered in consequence of the perpetration of a grave injustice and the damages that would be let loose by a war to repress the injustice. . . . There are greater evils than the physical death and destruction wrought in war. And there are human goods of so high an order that immense sacrifices may have to be borne in their defense." John Courtney Murray, S.J., "Morality and Modern War" (The Church Peace Union, 1959), p. 12. If the requirement of proportionality in legal doctrines of self-defense is not free from substantial ambiguity, the principle of proportion in traditional scholastic doctrine is so abstract as to have almost no apparent relevance.

[17] It will be apparent from the analysis given on preceding pages that the American just war doctrine has interpreted the requirement of proportionality largely in this latter sense.

[18] See pp. 122-27.

has passed only when the "aggressor" state no longer possesses the means with which to renew its unlawful conduct, or if not deprived entirely of these means, no longer possesses the means with which to renew its unlawful conduct with a reasonable prospect of success. With equal plausibility, it may be asserted that the danger remains as long as the "aggressor" government has not been removed from power. In this manner, doctrines of self-defense can be used, and have been used, to justify almost any use of force, whether limited or unlimited, and to effect an apparent reconciliation between the most varied of national interests and the "strictly preventive" purpose implicit in the requirement of proportionality.

It may of course be argued that given the circumstances attending the exercise of self-defense by nations, it is only reasonable that the requirement of proportionality should be interpreted as permitting the removal of the danger which initially justified the resort to measures of self-defense. Within domestic societies the state assures that a danger once repelled will be controlled. Hence the justification for the severe restriction of measures taken in self-defense is apparent. In the international society this assurance obviously cannot be given to nations, and an equally severe restriction of measures taken in self-defense is therefore unjustified. The argument is not without merit. But the dangers to which it gives rise are clear.

Nor is this all. Given the circumstances in which nations resort to force, it is hardly to be expected that measures allegedly taken in self-defense will be interpreted as serving only those restricted purposes that characterize the operation of self-defense within the state. To be sure, in resorting to the "defensive" employment of force, the nation will claim that it has acted for strictly preventive purposes. In almost the same breath, however, it will be asserted that force is employed to achieve order and justice for international society. The proverbial ease with which nations are able to reconcile these disparate claims testifies to the gulf that separates the operation of self-defense within the state from the operation of self-defense when left in the hands of nations. Still more relevant perhaps for the present inquiry is the significance of this identification in pointing up the unwillingness of nations even to profess with consistency, let alone to apply, a principle of self-defense drawn from the experience of domestic societies. In their insistence that they act not only on their own behalf but on behalf of the entire society of nations, nations arrogate to themselves the role of the state within domestic societies. Measures taken in self-defense are interpreted as "sanctions" and the state employing such force does so not merely for the "avoidance of evil" but for the "realization of right." Yet once force is endowed with the latter purpose, there are no discernible limits to the measures that may be taken in the guise of self-defense.[19]

These hazards do not arise merely because a "right" of self-defense is invoked within a system which still permits, in a negative sense at least, the "right" of self-judgment. Nor is their significance simply that of pointing up the need for the adjudication of claims of self-defense by an impartial organ representative of the international society. ". . . [W]hether action taken under the claim of self-defense was in fact aggressive or defensive," the Nuremberg Tribunal declared in a frequently cited passage of its judgment, "must

---

[19] It has been argued that the limits imposed by contemporary legal doctrines of self-defense are, in any event, quite tenuous. Still, there is a difference, in theory at least, between a concept of self-defense which enjoins a strictly preventive purpose and a concept of self-defense which has as its purpose the suppression of injustice and the realization of justice. The relevant point is that experience has demonstrated the almost congenital incapacity of nations to effect a separation between these two concepts. Logically, there is no necessity that a *bellum legale* of self-defense be transformed into a *bellum justum*. In practice, this transformation has occurred with a regularity that seems almost to suggest a necessary relationship.

ultimately be subject to investigation and adjudication if international law is ever to be enforced."[20] To assume that an impartial investigation and adjudication could "ultimately" be undertaken in the aftermath of conflict surely requires a very considerable feat of imagination, however, and a feat not made any easier by the example of Nuremberg. Presumably the difficulties raised by the attempt to apply a principle of self-defense to the behavior of nations would still remain. Thus the considerations that have impelled states in the past as well as in the present to expand indefinitely the limits of self-defense would continue to exert their influence. War would still remain the principal method by which the right of self-defense could be vindicated, and the actual course of hostilities would be no more amenable to control than in the past. Nor would there be any reason to expect that during hostilities the pretentious claims marked out by belligerents would prove any less excessive than in the past. Yet at the close of hostilities, the expectation is held out that the behavior of the belligerents would be subject to impartial investigation and adjudication and that this ultimate review would somehow inhibit future abuse of the right of self-defense.[21]

If the picture evoked by this prospect appears entirely incredible, it is because an important symptom has been mistaken for the whole disease. The hazards attending the application of the principle of self-defense to nations can

---

[20] Text in *American Journal of International Law*, XLI (1949), 207.

[21] In a recent inquiry into the legal issues attending the use of nuclear weapons in self-defense, the following masterpiece of understatement occurs: "Within so weak an international quasi-order as that of the United Nations, the question of action in self-defense is likely to remain one of auto-interpretation, at least until the struggle is decided. Even then, whatever the objective facts may be, the victor, if any, in a cosmic war between the two halves of a divided world would be unlikely to be marked with the stigma of aggression." Georg Schwarzenberger, *The Legality of Nuclear Weapons* (1958), pp. 39-40.

be overcome only by changes that would result in the radical transformation of the present international society. At the very least, that transformation would require a fundamental change in the possession and distribution of the means of coercion. The national state might remain, but it could no longer be the principal—let alone the sole—custodian of the instruments of violence. In the absence of such change, however, it is simply irrelevant to contend that the difficulties of applying the principle of self-defense follow from the nation's insistence upon a right of self-judgment, and that if this insistence were only to be once overcome the principle of self-defense would serve the ends of order and justice. For this assertion, if it is to prove relevant, must surely be considered in the context of the international society as it is presently organized and not as it might be ordered in accordance with an ideal scheme. To assert in the present context that the problems arising from the attempt to apply a principle of domestic order to the international society would not arise if the latter were only organized in a manner approximating the state merely expresses an irrelevant truism. One might just as well, though just as irrelevantly, point out that the considerations prompting the traditional justification of preventive war would not have arisen, and if arising would lack persuasiveness, in a society that possessed an order adequate to insure the security of its component parts.

Nor is it without significance that the one attempt in this century to realize a centralized system of international order and thereby to overcome the ambiguities and hazards inherent in contemporary doctrines of self-defense nevertheless sanctioned the preventive use of force subject to no substantive restraint other than that imposed by the necessity of obtaining the unanimity of the major powers. In the ideal scheme of order set forth in the Charter of the United Nations, the concept of preventive war is clearly implicit

in the powers accorded the Security Council. The Council
has only to decide upon the existence of a "threat to the
peace, breach of the peace, or act of aggression" before
taking the enforcement measures provided by the Charter.
These conditions are not further defined in the Charter,
and the evident intent of the principal framers, the Great
Powers, was to leave them conveniently vague. The Charter
provides no guarantee that the enforcement measures to be
taken by the Security Council must afford equal protection
to the legitimate interests of all member states. It is true
that the Security Council is obliged to act "in conformity
with the principles of justice and international law." This
injunction, which is not further elaborated by the Charter,
leaves the Great Powers at liberty to apply in a concrete
situation what they might consider to represent justice,
should they deem it inadvisable to apply existing law. Obviously, this requirement does not essentially affect the discretionary powers given the Council by the Charter. On
the contrary, the broad discretionary powers conferred upon
the Council by the Charter permit the interpretation that
preventive measures may be taken against a member state,
although the latter is acting only to preserve interests sanctioned by law and indeed interests upon which its security
depends.

Certainly the declared assumption of the Charter's principal framers was that the enforcement measures authorized
by the Charter were intended to preserve the legitimate
security interests of the individual member nations while
at the same time preserving the broader community interest
in maintaining international peace and order.[22] This assump-

---

[22] This assumption found an interesting reflection in the widely used
argument that if the permanent members were ever able to agree upon a
given course of action such agreement would prove possible only if governed
by principles generally recognized as just. The conclusion naturally follows
that if the Great Powers are able to agree in a concrete instance, justice as

tion cannot be dismissed simply as an ideological pretense designed to justify a system of order which guarantees only the interests of the Great Powers. Yet it is clear that the provisions of the Charter reflect the possibility that the price of order might necessitate the sacrifice by nations of what must otherwise be regarded as legitimate interests, the protection of which justifies the resort to force in self-defense. Thus the paradox inherent in the operation of the balance of power and manifested in one of the balance's most characteristic methods, preventive war, reappears in the order of collective security envisaged by the original Charter. If the preventive war sanctioned by the Charter is justified on the ground that force would be employed only for defensive purposes, the question must once again be raised: defensive for whom? In view of the express provisions of the Charter, the answer to this question has never permitted any real doubt.

These reflections are not made in order to condemn either the original order of the Charter or the justification of force

well as order is thereby insured. This argument provides a striking illustration of the perennial temptation to equate power and order with justice. That the equation is perhaps unconsciously made only renders it the more impressive. The cynic can be expected to conclude that if the powerful are once able to agree, one might as well consider such agreement as just, but it is always curious to find others embracing the same argument so readily. Yet this reaction to the Charter demonstrates, if further demonstration were needed, the almost congenital incapacity of men consciously to choose to subordinate the demands of justice to the requirements of order. Instead the two must somehow be reconciled, however spurious that reconciliation, and order endowed with the attribute of justice. No doubt the aspiration attending the framing of the Charter was that the Great Powers would insure not only order but justice as well, in the sense that the interests of the strong and the weak alike would be given equal consideration and treatment. The fact remains that the Charter's design of order was not made dependent in any meaningful way on the condition that the Great Powers would act justly but on the condition that they would retain a basic identity of interests, and that the order made possible by this identity of interests could be best insured by according the Security Council an essentially unlimited discretion.

that order implied; they are made to suggest that even a relatively centralized system of collective security cannot easily escape the moral hazards and ambiguities that have always attended attempts to justify the employment of force. Still less are these hazards and ambiguities to be avoided by contemporary doctrines of self-defense that confer upon states a discretion which is in substance just as broad, and therefore just as subject to abuse, as the discretion conferred by traditional doctrine. However justified the extension of the principle of self-defense may appear when applied to nations, it is those very circumstances in which it must be applied that render any extension hazardous. If the impact of state interest must prove unavoidably great, no matter how restrictive the interpretation given to the right of self-defense, to extend this right will inevitably incur the risk of foregoing any semblance of a claim to have placed substantive restrictions on the employment of force and to have established thereby a meaningful distinction between the legitimate and the illegitimate use of force. On the horns of this dilemma contemporary doctrines of self-defense have been impaled; they will continue to be impaled as long as international society retains the structural characteristics that have always marked it.

It is an illusion to believe that the ambiguities inherent in the traditional justification of preventive war are avoided in doctrines which give an extended interpretation to the right of self-defense. Is it any less an illusion to believe that no moral ambiguities mark a doctrine which insists that force ought to be employed only in response to force? Do restrictive interpretations of self-defense succeed in avoiding the dilemmas that have marked past justifications of force? In their purest form—though *only* in their purest form—restrictive doctrines of self-defense do resolve the problem of preventive war simply by forbidding altogether the anticipatory use of force. The right to employ force in self-defense is thus limited to the sole contingency of a prior armed attack. Hence, however injurious to a nation's vital interests the behavior of another state, the employment of force is nevertheless forbidden if such behavior itself falls short of the overt resort to force.[23]

It is by no means a decisive objection to restrictive doctrines of self-defense that the price to be paid for a consistent

---

[23] Advocacy of the restrictive interpretation of the right to use force in self-defense is normally attended by the claim that such an interpretation is required by the Charter of the United Nations. Although the evident intent of the Charter's framers was to restrict as much as possible the freedom of member-nations to employ force, a textual exegesis of the Charter's provisions does not necessitate the conclusion that the right to use force in self-defense is limited to the sole contingency of a prior "armed attack." The contrary conclusion depends upon a possible, though by no means a necessary, interpretation primarily of Art. 2, para. 4, obligating member states to "refrain in their international relations from the threat or use of force against the territorial integrity or political independence of any state, or in any other manner inconsistent with the purposes of the United Nations," and Art. 51, which declares that "Nothing in the present Charter shall impair the inherent right of individual or collective self-defense if an armed attack occurs against a Member of the United Nations, until the Security Council has taken the measures necessary to maintain international peace and security." Supporters of the restrictive interpretation insist that the qualification contained in Art. 2, para. 4 is merely a synonym for territorial inviolability and conclude that it is hardly possible to employ force, particularly within the territory of another state, without violating either territorial integrity, or political independence, or both. In opposition to this interpretation of Art. 2, para. 4, it has been asserted that force employed in legitimate self-defense cannot, by definition, be directed against another state's territorial integrity or political independence, and that consequently Art. 2, para. 4 does not affect the right to self-defense as a general principle of international law. With respect to Art. 51, the restrictive view is that the right to employ force in individual or collective defense against a prior "armed attack" is the sole exception to the general prohibition placed on the use of force by member states (except, of course, when taken in conformity with a Security Council decision). But if Art. 2, para. 4 is not read as a general prohibition on the use of force, even with respect to what formerly had been regarded as legitimate self-defense, Art. 51 leaves the traditional right of self-defense unimpaired.

As exercises in the art of legal interpretation both positions are persuasive, and without undue difficulty the Charter may be plausibly interpreted to adherence to them may prove very high.[24] But it is at least necessary to insist that the implications, both political and moral, that follow from this point not be neglected. For restrictive doctrines of self-defense may obviously result in denying to nations the only effective means of protecting their rights. The problem of preventive war may be resolved, at least in doctrine, but the solution may nonetheless appear unreasonable if it is inadequate for insuring the legitimate interests on which the security and independence of nations may rest. It is by now a commonplace that the methods characteristic of so-called "indirect aggression" need not involve the use of force, nor perhaps even the direct threat of force, though they may impair a state's independence as effectively as the classic method of overt military aggression. Restrictive doctrines of self-defense in denying to states the right to respond to such methods by employing, if necessary, forceful measures of self-defense may turn the right of political independence into little more than a sham.

To these hazards must be added the immeasurably greater risks imposed by the new technology. The latter evidently provides the strongest possible support for doctrines condemning the employment of force save in response to the prior use of force. Yet the new technology also furnishes impressive support for the preventive use of force. The reason for this is clear enough. The justification for restricting the use of force to the sole contingency of armed aggression has never rested simply upon the admitted moral hazards

support either position. But what is the utility of this continuing controversy over the "meaning" of the Charter? Is it not clear that the substantive questions at the basis of this controversy are of a moral and political character? The Charter, even if it were not vague and uncertain, cannot be expected to resolve these questions.

[24] The position that this is a decisive objection is set forth at considerable length by Julius Stone in his significant study, *Aggression and World Order* (1958). Although Professor Stone's efforts are directed to a critique of attempts to define aggression, his analysis is almost equally applicable to the task of defining self-defense.

invariably associated with the employment of force by nations. That justification has necessarily assumed that the first blow of an adversary could neither destroy nor seriously impair either the vital interests on behalf of which self-defense was to be exercised or the means for effectively exercising self-defense.

There have been periods when this assumption was not an unreasonable one for nations to make. Indeed, almost throughout this nation's history this assumption seemed not merely plausible but self-evident. It can no longer be made today, however. On the contrary, one of the few assumptions upon which a general consensus exists at present is that to concede the first blow to a nation armed with nuclear-missile weapons is to present a potential adversary with an advantage for which no parallel can be found in the history of warfare. Whether or not that advantage may prove decisive is a question whose very significance has fundamentall changed, because its relevance is now restricted primarily t the attacked state's strategic forces that may be expected to survive an initial strike. The question can have little rele vance to the task of directly protecting those other interest for which force has been defensively employed in the past since those other interests can no longer be protected in this traditional sense.[25] Instead, their protection must depend

---

[25] Thus Bernard Brodie writes: "Among the changes we have to cope with today, perhaps the most significant militarily is *the loss of the defensive function as an inherent capability of our major offensive forces.* These forces no longer interpose themselves between enemy and homeland, as armies did and still do whenever the chief burden of fighting is theirs. The force or forces that today pose the main deterrent threat are those comprised in and exemplified by the Strategic Air Command, which does not become a shield if deterrence fails. Although the counter-air or blunting mission of SAC is intended to achieve such protection, the success of that mission depends essentially on our having the initiative, more specifically, on our hitting first. It is not the only requirement, but it is the basic one. It is also the one least likely to be met." *Strategy in the Missile Age,* p. 225.

primarily on the aggressor's uncertainty about his capability to destroy all or a very high percentage of the enemy's strategic retaliatory forces and, of course, on the hope that an uncertain aggressor will therefore act rationally. But given circumstances in which a potential aggressor may have this capability, or circumstances in which a potential aggressor simply believes he possesses this capability, the effect of restrictive doctrines of self-defense may well require that nations refrain from the use of force until such time as they either no longer possess sufficient forces with which to protect their other interests or have no other interests left to protect.

One of the many paradoxes of self-defense doctrines in the nuclear-missile age, therefore, is that the more restrictive such doctrines are with respect to the circumstances in which force may be employed, the less possibility there may be that once force is employed it can serve a defensive purpose. Force can have a defensive purpose only when there are interests left to defend and enemy forces to threaten these interests. To the degree that either or both no longer exist, force may still have a purpose, but it is not defensive. For this reason the character of "pure" strategies of nuclear deterrence is profoundly ambivalent, their characterization depending upon whether one has in mind the purpose of the deterrent or the purpose of the action taken should the deterrent threat fail.[26]

26 In this connection Thomas C. Schelling has observed that "it is precisely the weapons with the most inhumane capabilities that a surprise-attack scheme seeks to preserve—namely, the weapons of retaliation, the weapons whose mission would be to punish rather than to fight. Deterrence of a major enemy assault depends mainly on weapons that threaten to *hurt* the enemy afterward, not to disarm him beforehand. A 'good' weapon— to push this philosophy all the way—is a weapon that can only hurt *people* and cannot possibly damage the other side's striking force; such a weapon is profoundly defensive in that it provides its possessor no incentive at all to strike first and initiate a major war." "Surprise Attack and Disarmament," in Klaus Knorr, ed., *NATO and American Security* (1959),

The purpose of calling attention to the obvious risks presented by these two extremes of indirect aggression and nuclear attack is not to condemn doctrines insistent upon forbidding the use of force save in response to the prior employment of force. Whether these doctrines are to be sanctioned or condemned is less relevant here than the recognition that nations, including this nation, remain unwilling to accept the possible consequences that may result from a rigorous and consistent adherence to so restrictive a standard. Yet once "reasonable" exceptions are made to this standard, once it is "interpreted" to permit the assimilation of circumstances considered tantamount to the use of force, the difficulties that were supposedly overcome inevitably reappear. To be sure, they may reappear in a doctrine that absolutely condemns preventive war. This does not make their reappearance any less real. Moral sentiment may insist that force be employed only in response to an armed attack. But, as has already been observed, only a modest amount of ingenuity is required to render the meaning of armed attack sufficiently broad to include a variety of forms of indirect aggression. And if the behavior encompassed by the concept of indirect aggression remains sufficiently obscure, it is difficult to see how these restrictive doctrines of self-defense have overcome the ambiguities inherent in the traditional justification for the preventive use of force.[27]

p. 179. But the "good" weapons Schelling describes are "profoundly defensive" only so long as they are not employed. Once employed, they undergo the most radical change in purpose. What is wholly defensive as a threat becomes wholly retributive as an actuality. On the other hand, weapons whose capabilities make them useful for preventive war (in Schelling's scheme weapons "that can exploit the advantage of striking first and consequently provide a temptation to do so") are less profoundly defensive as a deterrent but may still serve a defensive purpose if once employed in retaliation.

[27] Thus, to the American penchant for expanding the limits of the concept of armed attack may be added the position this nation has taken in United Nations discussions on the problem of defining aggression. The

Nor is it any less difficult to see how these ambiguities are avoided by the distinction increasingly drawn in recent years between a preventive war and a "pre-emptive" attack. The apparent purpose of this distinction is to reconcile the absolute condemnation of preventive war with the desire to avoid the consequences that might follow from such self-denial in the nuclear missile age.[28] Thus it is held that whereas a preventive war involves the deliberate and premeditated initiation of hostilities at the most propitious time, a pre-emptive attack involves an action in which the

substance of this position has been opposition to demands for defining aggression at the present juncture and, more significantly, a rejection of proposed definitions which would have the effect of identifying aggression simply with the first use of armed force. A reading of the various statements made over the past decade by American representatives both in the General Assembly's International Law Commission and in the Assembly itself affords no clear indication of the acts which might be encompassed within the American concept of aggression. It is not even clear whether the American position assumes that force may be legitimately employed against any and all acts of aggression. About all that is clear from the record of these discussions is that this nation considers the concept of aggression, however undefinable, to be of critical importance and that at least against some forms of aggression the employment of force evidently constitutes the lawful exercise of self-defense.

[28] A recent report of the House Appropriations Committee has endorsed the idea of a pre-emptive attack in the following terms: "In the final analysis, to effectively deter a would-be aggressor, we should maintain our armed forces in such a way and with such an understanding that should it ever become obvious that an attack upon us or our allies is imminent, we can launch an attack before the aggressor has hit either us or our allies. This is an element of deterrence which the United States should not deny itself. No other form of deterrence can be relied upon." House Committee on Appropriations report, *Department of Defense Appropriation Bill, 1961* (86th Cong., 2nd Sess.) , p. 8.

It is noteworthy that the capability of undertaking successful pre-emptive attack is regarded here simply as a necessary "element of deterrence." The justification for maintaining that capability and for invoking it in the appropriate circumstances is therefore assimilated to the justification given to the strategy of deterrence generally, i.e., its purely defensive character. Obviously, a deterrent strategy will prove more effective if a attempt is made to seize the initiative from an adversary who has either already resorted to force or is certain to initiate hostilities in the immediate future. Obviously, if an adversary has already initiated hostilities it no longer remains possible either to prevent or to pre-empt him in the use of force. But one may still pre-empt the adversary in taking certain measures, and notably in pre-empting him in the strategic employment of nuclear weapons. If the strategic employment of nuclear weapons is undertaken after an enemy has initiated hostilities, though before he has resorted to the strategic use of nuclear weapons, then the term "pre-emptive attack" can only indicate the first strategic use of nuclear weapons. There is clearly no justification for assuming, however, that the adversary's initiation of hostilities thereby indicates his intent to undertake a strategic air attack as well, for this assumption implies that the adversary is deliberately inviting a pre-emptive nuclear attack. If anything, it is precisely the contrary assumption that appears more reasonable.[29] But the element of compulsion presumed

potential aggressor can be persuaded not only that an attack would bring forth certain retaliation in kind but that the intended victim may even be able to anticipate an aggressive attack and take effective preventive measures. It should be equally apparent, however, that the capability to conduct a successful pre-emptive war may serve other than purely defensive purposes.

[29] In this connection, Bernard Brodie (*Strategy in the Missile Age*, p. 242) writes that: "The distinguishing characteristic of the idea, which has been called 'pre-emptive attack,' is that it envisages a strategic air attack by the United States upon the Soviet Union only after the latter has already set in motion its own strategic air attack, but *before* that attack is consummated and preferably before it gets well under way." If the strategic employment of nuclear weapons is undertaken only after an enemy "has already set in motion" his own strategic air attack, then the term pre-emptive attack is surely misleading from every point of view. Nor is it explained how, even in theory, a strategic air attack can be set in motion and yet a counter-attack somehow carried out before the initial attack "gets well under way." Brodie notes that "unkind critics" have referred to the idea of pre-emptive attack as the philosophy of "I won't strike first unless you do," and sug-

to attend a pre-emptive attack is supposely lacking in a preventive war situation. For then, the argument runs, a nation is still free to choose alternatives other than force, and for this reason the choice of violence must be condemned. In undertaking a pre-emptive attack a nation is no longer free to choose other courses of action. It acts in a situation of necessity, and this necessity allegedly provides its justification. The "necessity" that attends a pre-emptive attack and that provides its justification is therefore held to be an exception, although presumably a very limited exception, to the assumptions otherwise informing the American interpretation of international conflict.

Yet it is clear that whatever the terminology employed, a pre-emptive attack is unavoidably a form of preventive war if it implies the initial use of force. The distinction drawn between a preventive war and a pre-emptive attack can hardly be interpreted other than as an acknowledgment, however indirect and evasive, that there are preventive wars and preventive wars, some apparently justified and others unjustified. To be sure, this conclusion must prove unpalatable to a doctrine so insistent upon the absolute rejection of preventive war. For this reason it is asserted that even if the idea of a pre-emptive attack may be considered a form of preventive war, it still represents no more than the barest concession to an otherwise immoral principle. The concession is so restricted, though so evidently required for survival in the nuclear age, that it cannot reasonably be compared either with the traditional meaning given the odious principle or with the consequences that have always attended its application. But it is precisely the implications of the new technology that can be used to challenge this argument.

gests that the phrase should be amended to read "unless you attempt to" (p. 242). The criticism may be unkind, but Brodie's instructive analysis of the difficulties attending a pre-emptive attack supports the conclusion that it is not essentially incorrect.

The "necessity" that is held to justify a pre-emptive attack can no longer be regarded as stemming from a situation both exceptional in occurrence and readily identifiable as a distinct series of acts; in the final analysis, this necessity stems less from the overt behavior of a potential adversary armed with nuclear-missile weapons than from the mere fact that the adversary possesses the means to destroy with almost no advance warning. Nor, as already observed, is it reasonable to assume that if the potential adversary should determine to initiate an attack, he would do so only after indicating his intentions through overt action. On the contrary, he must have every possible reason for refraining from any action that would afford the least indication of his intentions. Against another state armed with nuclear-missile weapons, the display of such intentions would represent the extreme limits of irrational behavior.[30]

It is, therefore, the very existence of the new technology that constitutes the essence of the "necessity" held to justify a pre-emptive attack. But if this is true, what are the limits to the application of a strategy of pre-emptive attack? If a nation is placed in constant danger of destruction without advance warning, when is a pre-emptive attack not justified? These questions cannot be turned aside simply by pointing once again to the hazards incurred if the idea of pre-emptive attack is clearly abandoned. They must instead be answered by demonstrating that the justification given for pre-emptive attack somehow avoids the ambiguities and possibilities for misuse inherent in the traditional justification of preventive war. A persuasive demonstration to this effect has yet to be made. Indeed, the irony of this attempt to save only the

---

[30] This does not, of course, preclude the possibility that a nation might manifest such irrational behavior. It is merely suggested that it would be absurd to base the idea of pre-emptive attack—and indirectly at least, the justification for undertaking a pre-emptive attack—on the assumption that nations will act in so irrational a manner.

"purest residue" of the traditional justification of preventive war must be apparent. When applied to the realities of the new technology this purest residue not only conspicuously fails to resolve the perennial moral hazards attending the preventive use of force but becomes the starting point for the creation of new moral dilemmas.

It will not do, then, to condemn the traditional justification for preventive war by pointing to the gulf that separated doctrine from the actuality of state practice, while refusing to make the same contrast between ideal and reality in the case of current notions of self-defense. The most telling criticism of the traditional doctrine was that it always remained vague enough to be compatible with almost any policy. In consequence, a clear disparity between doctrine and practice could hardly have arisen. The preceding pages have sought to show, however, that it would be rash to assume that a similar criticism cannot be brought against contemporary doctrines of self-defense. Once these make even the slightest departures from the rigid confines of the norm prescribing that force should be employed only in response to the prior use of force, they are inevitably enmeshed in the same difficulties that have always marked the justification given for the preventive use of force. Admittedly, these ambiguities can be overcome by a doctrine that forbids the resort to force altogether, save for the sole contingency of a prior armed attack. But the price that might have to be paid by nations consistently conforming to so restrictive a standard might prove very high. And quite apart from the willingness of nations to conform to this standard, the abuses to which the traditional justification for preventive war gave rise can be overcome only by opening the way to new inequities. In denying to nations the instrument of force without providing an effective alternative for insuring their security and independence, restrictive doctrines of self-defense may represent neither a contribution to the requirements of order nor a fulfillment of the demands of justice.

Yet even if the criteria of effectiveness and moral relevance are put aside, there remains the consideration that so-called restrictive doctrines of self-defense are clearly restrictive only in the sense that they forbid the prior resort to armed force. The host of moral problems that invariably attends the actual employment of force, problems that concern the manner in which force should be employed as well as the purposes for which force should be exercised, are no more satisfactorily resolved by restrictive doctrines than they are by extended interpretations of the right of self-defense. In either case, the manner and purpose of war remain vague and, consequently, easily subject to abuse. If it is an exaggeration to single out contemporary doctrines of self-defense, whether restrictive or extended, as leading inevitably to the revival of the idea of punitive war, it does at least seem clear that there is little in such doctrines to prevent the conduct of what is, in fact if not in name, a punitive war. No doubt it is true that in the formal sense doctrines of self-defense must disavow such a purpose. But the distinction between the strictly preventive purpose that forms the essential feature of self-defense and the retributive purpose that exceeds the limits of self-defense is easier to state as an abstract proposition than to apply to the complex circumstances of international conflict. And even on the level of pure theory it is a distinction by no means free of ambiguities. Indeed, it is these very ambiguities that give a semblance of plausibility to the justification of wars which, however defensive in their immediate origin, are fought without substantial limitation either in the manner of employing force or in the purposes sought through force.

IV

It is tempting to see in the American attitude toward preventive war the reflection of an awareness of the moral risks incurred once force is employed by nations. These risks are bound to prove considerable even in relatively favorable circumstances, let alone in the circumstances presently attending the use of force. The only certainty once force is employed is the destruction of values. Against this certainty can be placed only the possibility—it is never more than a possibility—that the values to be preserved through force will somehow justify the suffering and destruction caused by war.

Yet it does not follow that the moral risks incurred by nations employing force necessarily condemn preventive war under any and all circumstances.[31] That war has served more often as an instrument of injustice than of justice, that it is not the vindication of justice war assures but the triumph of the stronger over the weaker, and that the conditions which have always marked the employment of force by nations only insure that force will prove a useful instrument to the strong, are considerations which, even if accepted without reservations, do not compel the conclusion

---

[31] Though it does follow that a heavy burden rests on those who do initiate the use of force. Of course, it is easy enough to point to the consequences of renouncing the preventive use of force. It is no less easy, however, to point to the acts that have been reconciled with doctrines freely sanctioning the preventive use of force. The argument that in the absence of institutions to preserve order and to insure a "minimal" justice nations must be permitted to protect their interests as best they can, if need be through the instrument of force, is based on the assumption that the misuse and consequent injustice to which the exercise of this extreme form of self-redress may give rise are less to be feared than the inequities to which its severe restriction may lead. At the very least, that assumption does not spring self-evidently from the history of international conflict. If anything, it is the contrary assumption this history suggests.

that nations are never justified in initiating the use of force. No doubt, these considerations emphasize the moral hazards of resorting to force and, beyond this, the desirability of reducing, as far as possible, the role and importance of force.[32] Still, their immediate relevance to the concrete circumstances that mark the historic rivalries of nations is not self-evident and should not be exaggerated. Whether or not the initiation of force may find a justification in a given instance remains dependent upon a weighing of the risks force may involve against the values that may have to be sacrificed by abstaining from force.

If these considerations are nevertheless found to condemn the preventive use of force at the present juncture, such condemnation must be based on the consequences expected to follow from the employment of force. If preventive war, for whatever reason, is to be rejected, such rejection must proceed from the conviction that in view of the expected consequences force can no longer serve either as an instrument of justice or of order. The significance of this renunciation of force should not be misunderstood. It does not, or at least it need not, imply that the renunciation of force, even if effective, would thereby guarantee the security of nations, but only that the degree of security which would follow would prove greater than what could be expected if states were to remain free to employ force whenever they conceived their interests to so require. Nor does this conviction suggest that the renunciation of force is to be equated

---

[32] It is equally apparent, however, that these considerations can scarcely be reconciled with a doctrine that is complacent about the manner and purposes of a "defensive" war. Still less may these considerations be reconciled with the morally complacent conviction that whatever the lessons of the past "in this particular instance" force undoubtedly serves as an instrument of justice. The consequences to which this conviction may lead those who are persuaded that their defensive response to aggression thereby resolves all the moral dilemmas attending the employment of force have been noted elsewhere in this essay.

with justice, but only that the injustice resulting from the employment of force will prove greater than the injustice suffered by the refusal to resort to this extreme form of self-redress. The essential point is that in the present circumstances, the insecurity and injustice expected to follow from the use of force is considered to outweigh the values to be preserved through force. It is clear that this position is necessarily dependent upon certain assumptions regarding the nature of warfare in the nuclear age, assumptions whose validity need not, and indeed cannot, be accepted simply on faith.[33] Yet the relevant question here is not the validity of these assumptions but the justification that may be given even for the "defensive" employment of force once they are accepted.

In the various forms this nation's policy of nuclear deterrence has taken over the past decade, it has never demonstrated a tender regard for the consequences expected to follow from the defensive employment of force. On the contrary, it has consistently manifested a striking insensitivity—at least a striking verbal insensitivity—on this score. The principal justification for deterrence, and particularly for the more extreme versions of deterrence, has not been based on the consequences envisaged by the deterrent threat but rather on the expectation that the deterrent threat would never have to be carried out. Indeed, to the degree that this expectation came to form the obsessive preoccupation of American policy, the result has been to abstract the elementary logic of deterrence from other modifying considerations

---

[33] Thus the principal assumption on which this position must rest is simply that any resort to force exceeding the level of a mere "brush fire" or minor border skirmish and involving nuclear powers either directly or indirectly will in all probability eventuate in a conflict marked by the strategic employment of nuclear weapons. The phrase "strategic employment of nuclear weapons" can cover a multitude of sins, but at the very least it must imply the use of nuclear weapons for the purpose of destroying an enemy's strategic forces.

and simply to regard the effectiveness of deterrence as directly proportionate to the horrendous character of the deterrent threat.

In a significant sense, it is true that the consequences envisaged by the deterrent threat, especially in its more extreme interpretations, have been endowed with an almost unreal quality. The emphasis of deterrence—its "reality" so to speak—has always been the threat, as is indicated by the finality with which the official expositors of deterrence have referred to any major aggression as the "failure" of that policy. Nevertheless, should the unexpected occur, the failure of deterrence has never been regarded as a moral failure. For the policy of deterrence has been based throughout upon the conviction that whatever the consequences the "defensive" employment of force in response to armed aggression is justified. It is precisely this conviction, however, which must prove difficult, if not impossible, to reconcile with a condemnation of preventive war stemming from the considerations sketched out above. These considerations do not call into question merely the justification for initiating the use of force. They must equally call into question the justification for responding to the aggressive use of force if the consequences of employing force are such that war can no longer serve as an instrument of justice. Even a defensive war may no longer be a just war once these considerations are accepted.

Against this view it has been urged that the stringent requirements of defense simply no longer permit the strict observance of many traditional restraints placed on the conduct of warfare, that although a defensive war must still be regarded as a just war, these restraints must be adjusted to, and in effect made subordinate to, the necessities imposed by the new technology. It is apparent that the policy of deterrence and the doctrine informing this policy have gone very far in endorsing the argument that the justice of war is not essentially affected by the weapons and methods employed in warfare. But if this argument is accepted, it is at least necessary to acknowledge the consequences that follow from it. In the nuclear age, its acceptance must emphasize that there are virtually no substantive restraints which need be observed by those waging a defensive war.

The reluctance to admit the consequences of this argument is readily understandable.[34] Sensitive consciences continue to call attention to a tradition, both Christian and humanitarian, that requires the observance of at least certain minimal restraints in the conduct of warfare. Although a defensive war may be regarded as a just war, and those waging it may be permitted to employ means appropriate

---

[34] This reluctance has characterized many admirable efforts to come to grips with the moral dilemmas posed by nuclear warfare. Thus Reinhold Neibuhr and Angus Dun have insisted that: "The notion that the excessive violence of atomic warfare has ended the possibility of a just war does not stand up. . . . The moral problem has been altered, not eliminated. . . . The consequences of a successful defense are fearful to contemplate, but the consequences of a successful aggression, with the tyrannical monopoly of the weapons of mass destruction, are calculated to be worse. While the avoidance of excessive and indiscriminate violence, and of such destruction as would undermine the basis for future peace remain moral imperatives in a just war, it does not seem possible to draw a line in advance, beyond which it would be better to yield than to resist." "God Wills Both Justice and Peace" *Christianity and Crisis,* June 13, 1955, p. 78. No doubt the "excessive violence of atomic warfare" has not ended the possibility of a just war, if one assumes the continued possibility of defensive wars other than atomic or even of wars in which atomic weapons are used only for tactical purposes. We are considering the extreme case, however, since it is the strategic employment of nuclear weapons that constitutes the limiting case and poses the critical dilemmas. If the avoidance of excessive and indiscriminate violence remains a moral imperative in a just war, does the prospect held out by the strategic employment of nuclear weapons, even though used only in response to overt armed aggression, end the possibility of a just war? If not, is it meaningful to speak of any substantive restraints which remain to limit the conduct of a just war? And in view of the expected duration of hostilities marked from the outset by the strategic employment of nuclear weapons, if a line is not to be drawn in advance, is it reasonable to assume that it will ever be drawn?

to the purpose of such a war, we are nevertheless reminded that even a defensive war must observe certain restraint. But what are the limitations that must be observed in a nuclear conflict, and how relevant are they in delineating meaningful limitations on the conduct of warfare? Surely it is not sufficient simply to insist that the employment of nuclear weapons must be governed by the strict requirements of defense, when it is precisely the awesome measures that may be required even in a defensive war which constitute the main source of the dilemma.

It is of course quite true that the possibility of imposing substantive limitations upon the conduct of war has always depended in large measure on the renunciation of grandiose purposes and the acceptance of discrete and limited objectives. Yet it is a mistake to assume that the acceptance of limited objectives must insure the limitation of force as well—that there is a necessary relation between the limitation of the purposes sought in war and the limitation of the manner of warfare. The possibility that force may be employed with reasonable discrimination in a defensive war, however narrowly the purpose of defense is initially restricted, will still depend upon other circumstances—for example, the enemy's purposes in war and the manner in which he pursues these purposes. That possibility must also depend upon the nature of the weapons with which the war is fought, and, in this sense at least, it may not be misleading to speak of a "necessity" that inheres in technology. A nation may perceive the dangers of complacently identifying its purposes with the imperative requirements of the moral law and abstain from equating defensive wars with an insistence upon the aggressor's unconditional surrender. Even so, it may still use nuclear weapons that wreak destruction that is of an indiscriminate character.[35]

[35] A recent study on the limitation of war in the nuclear age declares that "the use of armaments should be separated from ideological sys-

There remains the position that whatever the alleged necessities of defense in the nuclear age, the conduct of a just war must nevertheless conform at least to those elemental restraints which spring from the imperative requirements of humanity. Nothing can justify either the deliberate abandonment of the effort to apply force in a discriminating manner or the use of weapons whose very nature removes any doubt that they can be applied with discrimination.

tems . . . there is no ground for Christians to support a war for the objective of unconditional surrender . . . if ideological causes and unconditional surrender are removed as legitimate objectives, there remains the possibility of using armaments in order to push an aggressor to the point where he is willing to negotiate. The aggression must be halted or repelled, and a cease fire arranged as soon as there is willingness to negotiate on this basis. . . . It is admitted that even this limited objective might permit a considerable war. Given, however, the present military and political situation, it is hard to see how the objectives of war can be further limited without disregarding all legitimate considerations of defense and order within the world of nations. Such an objective is, in contrast to all out war, a discriminating objective." "Christians and the Prevention of War in An Atomic Age—A Theological Discussion" (World Council of Churches—Division of Studies, 1958), pp. 33-34. No doubt the objective of war proposed in this study is limited and discriminating. Yet it cannot thereby insure that the means employed to achieve that objective will be discriminating. Whether or not the means will prove discriminating must depend upon the limits directly imposed on the means themselves. In this latter respect, the study declares that the "all out use of these [nuclear] weapons should never be resorted to," though it purposely "refrains from defining the stage at which all out war may be reached" (p. 30). Elsewhere, the study urges the development of "that discipline which is determined to use the possession of megaton weapons and the upper ranges of kiloton weapons as deterrents only, and only in a discriminating way. It is supremely important that there be a disciplined use of the deterrent value of existing weapons. They must be used for the discriminate objectives which we have mentioned, and for no others" (p. 35). These injunctions are not free from ambiguity, however, since there is a distinction—and in the nuclear age a perhaps vital distinction—between the discriminating use of weapons and their employment for discriminate objectives. The contrast drawn between an undefined "all out war" and the discriminate objective of halting or repelling aggression may only serve to obscure this critical, yet unresolved, dilemma.

Thus the deliberate attack upon cities made with the primary intent to kill or to terrorize civilian populations is forbidden under any circumstances,[36] as is the use of weapons which altogether escape the control of those who employ them.[37] The evident implication is that as long as these irreducible requirements are complied with, a defensive war may still be considered a just war.

[36] This familiar injunction formed one of the high points of the report entitled "The Struggle for World Community," issued by the Second Assembly of the World Council of Churches held at Evanston in August 1954. Recognizing the "right of national self-defense" the report declared: "Christians should urge that both the United Nations and their own governments limit military action strictly to the necessities of international security. Yet even this is not enough. The Churches must condemn the deliberate mass destruction of civilians in open cities by whatever means and for whatever purposes." The experience of World War II has already demonstrated the futility of this pathetic effort to apply to aerial warfare some remnant of the traditional principle distinguishing between combatants and noncombatants. The bombing of military objectives resulting in "incidental" though unintentional injury to the civilian population and bombing with the intent to terrorize the civilian population became a distinction without a practical difference—a consequence reflected after the war in the significant absence of any war crimes trials in which the accused were charged with terror bombing of civilian populations or simply with the indiscriminate bombardment of cities. Given the consequences that followed from the employment of "iron bombs," what can be expected from the strategic employment of nuclear-missile weapons? To be sure, belligerents will not, at least they need not, concede that the obliteration of cities was ever deliberate, that it was ever intended to disrupt and to terrorize the civilian population. There will always be objectives in or near urban centers that the belligerent may claim to be of sufficient military importance to justify attacking. Will it make any material difference if cities are deliberately destroyed or simply destroyed incidentally to the attack upon what is claimed to be a legitimate military objective?

[37] In his engrossing essay on "Morality and Modern War" (p. 13) Father Murray cites a statement of Pius XII in which the legitimacy of employing nuclear weapons is limited to the "strict exigencies of defense." The Pope went on to declare that "when the employment of this means entails such an extension of the evil that it entirely escapes from the control of man, its use ought to be rejected as immoral. Here it is no longer a question of defense against injustice and of the necessary safeguard of legitimate possessions, but of the annihilation, pure and simple, of all human life

It is a mark of the desperate pass to which we have been brought that any comfort may be derived from this position.[38] Yet its most depressing feature is not the negligible prospect that in a nuclear conflict belligerents will observe the restraints it enjoins, but that belligerents may have very little need ever to deny these vague and obscure prohibitions. In view of the extent to which the imperative requirements of humanity have already been adjusted to the necessities of defensive wars fought with conventional weapons, there is little reason to assume that these requirements may not be stretched still further and adjusted to the necessities imposed by a defensive war fought with nuclear weapons. To believe that the imperative requirements of humanity may be invoked to preserve even a semblance of the traditional distinction drawn between military objectives and the civilian population of an enemy borders on an illusion, an illusion that serves only to obscure further the moral predicament posed by nuclear weapons.

within its radius of action. This is not permitted on any account." Father Murray, while acknowledging that this is an "extremely broad statement," insists that: "We have here an affirmation . . . of the rights of innocence, of the distinction between combatant and noncombatant." But what is the relevance of this affirmation in setting meaningful limits to the conduct of nuclear war? The distinction between combatants and noncombatants may surely be destroyed without employing weapons whose effects "entirely escape from the control of man," whatever that obscure and tortured phrase may mean. Besides, to declare that nuclear weapons may be used but to insist that the annihilation of all human life within their radius of action is not permitted comes very close to forbidding what in the same breath has been permitted.

[38] Nevertheless, a distinguished international jurist, after chiding his brethren for neglecting the realities of the new weapons of mass destruction and for persisting in the futile enterprise of "restating" the traditional law of war in the nuclear age, can write: "The only laws that preserve their imprescriptible authority are the unwritten ones dictated by respect for the principles of humanity. It is directly upon these that the safeguards of the future must be built." Charles de Visscher, *Theory and Reality in Public International Law* (1957), p. 293.

These reflections have assumed that a conflict in which nuclear weapons are used without any assurance of substantive restraints may still be considered a defensive war. Is this assumption justified? No doubt, the answer must seem self-evident to those who insist upon identifying the character of war with the circumstances marking the initiation of hostilities. Once this identification is accepted, the manner of employing force is by definition defensive in nature provided that force is employed only in response to armed aggression. Nor does it make an essential difference whether the specific purpose sought in responding to aggression is to repel the enemy, to disarm him, or to annihilate him, for all three purposes must be deemed compatible with a defensive war. It is this identification, buttressed by the conviction that the American purpose simply precludes anything other than a strictly defensive war, which has facilitated in the past the easy acceptance even of extreme versions of nuclear deterrence. Thus the policy of "massive retaliation" has been generally interpreted as serving the obviously defensive purpose of preventing armed aggression and, should deterrence fail, the equally obvious purpose of waging a defensive war. That purpose has therefore been held to confer upon peace-loving nations the right not only to threaten potential aggressors with a degree of retaliation far in excess of the force required to repel an aggression but to carry out that threat if expedient. Indeed, until very recently at least, the infrequent criticism that this marked disparity between the evil to be prevented and the Draconian retaliatory measures threatened could only mean that American policy relied upon a threat carrying radically aggressive implications for both the conduct and purposes of war was dismissed as perverse. As long as this nation retained, or was thought to retain, an overwhelming superiority in nuclear weapons and their means of delivery, these implications troubled very few consciences; a threat which envisaged the possible annihilation of an aggressor was readily accepted as having a strictly defensive character and therefore as fully consonant with the moral law. Morality required only that this nation or its allies receive the first blow, though not the first decisive blow. The strategy of deterrence has assumed throughout that the decisive blow would be the act of retaliation. In this manner, the moral law would be observed and at the same time military success would be guaranteed; a defensive war according to the moral law would still reap the military advantages otherwise attending a decisive preventive strike.[39]

It should give pause for reflection that an increased concern over the justification for employing nuclear weapons has not been unrelated to the increasing nuclear capability of the potential adversary and to an appreciation that the threat of massive nuclear retaliation is no longer unilateral. Given the prospect of a conflict in which both sides are equally endowed with nuclear weapons and their means of delivery, the once easy assumptions on which deterrence rested and from which it drew much of its moral complacency must become progressively difficult to sustain. The reasons for this are clear enough. Against an adversary pos-

---

[39] In discussing the limits of a war of defense Herbert Butterfield has referred to cases of defensive treaties with an offensive *arrière-pensée*. *Christianity, Diplomacy and War* (1953), p. 19. In much the same sense deterrence—and particularly the more extreme version of deterrence—has been a defensive policy with an offensive *arrière-pensée*. Butterfield points out that "though your enemy may have attacked you first, and you have a right to defend yourself, his sin does not itself justify you in becoming an aggressor at his expense—does not justify you in carrying on the war for the purpose of destroying that enemy or breaking him up." But these words may be lost on a doctrine that views the response to aggression as necessarily defensive, and consequently sanctioned by the moral law, whatever the precise character this response may take. Thus, however aggressive in other respects, massive retaliation has always been regarded from a moral point of view as purely defensive. The same reasoning that has informed massive retaliation finds a lingering echo in the concept of pre-emptive attack, though here it is strained to the point of incredulity.

sessed of roughly equal capabilities for destruction, the use of nuclear weapons can serve a defensive purpose only as long as the possibility exists that they may be employed to disarm the enemy of the means with which to accomplish your destruction. Even at present this possibility must probably be regarded as distinctly limited, and with the passage of time the expectation is that it will become still more remote. Yet to the degree that it does remain a distinct possibility it is necessarily dependent on the condition that force will be used preventively in every sense of the term. A doctrine insistent upon identifying the defensive character of a war with the circumstances in which violence is initiated can have almost no prospect of disarming an opponent. The latter by the very act of initiating a nuclear conflict will have disarmed himself of at least a large portion of his strategic forces. In so doing he may succeed either in effectively disarming his victim or in accomplishing a sufficient level of general destruction to leave his victim with very little worth defending.

Nor is this all. If the possibility of waging a defensive nuclear war requires the initiation of force, it also suggests that the employment of force may require a level of destruction that encompasses not only the disarming of the enemy but very likely the substantial destruction of his major cities as well. To be sure, the destruction of an enemy's cities need not form a deliberate purpose; it could merely prove incidental to the task of insuring that the enemy is left with the minimum of strategic forces with which to retaliate—and, ideally, with no strategic forces at all. If in order to destroy the greatest possible percentage of an enemy's retaliatory forces a large number of targets must be attacked, a nation undertaking a preventive strike cannot be expected to refrain from so doing simply because some of these targets are in the proximity of population centers. Such restraint may of course be exercised out of fear that the injured enemy would otherwise have no reason to refrain from retaliating, with whatever forces remaining at his disposal, against the major cities of the nation making the initial attack. But he may do this in any event. With the sharply reduced forces which would remain at his disposal it will prove very difficult to concentrate with any real prospect of success against targets that may already be deprived of their former value and that are, in any case, now too numerous to attack. In these circumstances, the nation suffering the preventive strike may be confronted with the choice either of concentrating its remaining forces against the enemy's cities or of doing nothing at all. It is possible that with the threat of a second attack directed exclusively against its cities the injured nation might choose to do nothing at all. Obviously, this possibility must be regarded by the nation waging a preventive strike as extremely risky, and rightly so. Yet the only alternative is a preventive strategy that deliberately seeks to "overkill" the enemy's retaliatory forces, with the hope that these forces can be reduced to tolerable proportions. It is difficult to see how this strategy could be effectively carried out save by an attack which would in its effects, if not in its intent, border on indiscriminate destruction.

It will be replied that such a preventive strategy perverts the very meaning of defense, that it seeks to present in the guise of a defensive war what is in reality the most radically aggressive war man has yet conceived, and that its acceptance affords a standard excuse for undertaking a war of annihilation. Whatever the merit of this response, and it is not to be lightly dismissed, the moral paradoxes raised by nuclear conflict are not satisfactorily resolved simply by applying considerations relevant to traditional forms of warfare. It is easy enough to continue to stress the desirability of confining a defensive war to the restricted purpose of "halting" or "repelling" an aggressor. But what is the possible relevance of this admonition when applied to the circumstances of a general nuclear conflict? Does the picture that is evoked by these terms have any relevance when applied to the circumstances marking the outset of nuclear warfare? How does one halt or repel an aggressor if the initial act of aggression is also likely to be the decisive act?

More relevant, perhaps, is the stricture enjoining the disarming of an enemy rather than the indiscriminate destruction of his cities and population. Yet if this imperative remains tied to a doctrine which condemns the preventive use of force, it has, for reasons already noted, almost no chance of realization. And even if the aggressor's initial strike were to leave the victim with a substantial portion of retaliatory forces intact, the task of disarming the aggressor of his remaining forces would still raise substantially the same problems considered above in relation to a preventive strike. The same, or very nearly the same, moral risks of imposing indiscriminate destruction must be assumed in undertaking a retaliatory strike as are assumed in attempting to disarm the enemy through a clearly preventive strike. If anything, the relatively unfavorable circumstances in which the task of attempting to disarm the enemy is now undertaken can only serve to increase those risks.

The possibility must therefore be faced that adherence to a doctrine insistent upon the renunciation of preventive war may not permit in the circumstances marking nuclear conflict either the repelling or the disarming of the aggressor. What then is the purpose served by retaliating against an aggressor who, by the initial act of resorting to aggression, has succeeded in destroying both a very substantial portion of the victim's retaliatory forces and urban centers? Indeed, why strike back at all? Can the act of retaliation be regarded as an act of defense, particularly if it is primarily directed, as in all probability it would be, against the aggressor's cities? No doubt, when measured by the depth of the conviction that the act of retaliation would necessarily possess a defensive character, these questions must seem absurd. Their apparent absurdity is a significant indication of the extent to which the character and purpose of the action to be taken should deterrence once fail have always been identified with the purpose of the deterrent threat. That identification is profoundly in error. However defensive in character the threat to destroy an enemy's cities only as an act of retaliation, the carrying out of that threat is anything but defensive.[40] If such a retaliatory measure has any purpose at all other than one of pure retribution, it is simply to prevent the aggressor from inheriting the earth.

[40] Once again, the paradox earlier noted (pp. 138-40) must be emphasized. The more purely defensive the deterrent threat as a threat, the less likelihood there is that this threat can serve a defensive purpose should the need ever arise to act upon it. The moral issues raised by a purely deterrent posture are discussed in succeeding pages.

III

On Banishing Force
from History

F THE ANALYSIS SUGGESTED IN THE PRECEDING PAGES is substantially correct, nuclear-missile weapons hold out the prospect of conflict which may be neither subject to restraint nor meaningfully described as defensive. Can such a war be justified? If not, is there nevertheless a justification for threatening to wage such a war? Can there be a moral sanction for threatening to take a measure which, if circumstances ever required carrying it out, could find no justification?

The recognition of moral dilemmas in statecraft involves more than simply the recognition of a tension between moral aspiration and the realities of political life. That tension, resulting in an awareness of the moral imperfections that characterize man's collective relations, will cause an uneasy conscience but it need not give rise to moral dilemmas. Moral dilemmas are the product of conflicting, though equally compelling, moral demands and the inability of the individual to resolve this conflict satisfactorily. Thus the peculiar poignancy marking the moral dilemma is not to be found either in the degree to which action may deviate from the ethical standard that ought to govern it or even in the sacrifice of value that critical political decisions almost invariably entail.[1] Instead, it is to be found in a funda-

---

[1] It is this sacrifice of value that marks the choice of either action as tragic. Thus the decision to resort to force may be seen as tragic if only

mental uncertainty over the justification for choosing any of the alternative courses of action that remain open.

To be sure, it is always possible—indeed, it is quite normal—that men will entertain potentially irreconcilable moral demands and that circumstances will nevertheless not compel them to choose between these demands. The security of the nation may be regarded as an absolute value. At the same time, preventive war may be absolutely condemned. The moral law may sanction a war of defense against armed aggression, but the same moral law may also impose restraints on the manner in which even defensive wars may be fought. The survival of the nation may be justified largely in terms of the transcendent values embodied in the nation. Nevertheless, the physical survival of the nation may itself be considered a good which justifies the taking of any measures, regardless of the possible consequences such measures may have for the world at large. There is no assurance that these moral demands—and still others—can always be reconciled. Whether or not they will be reconciled, if indeed they can be, necessarily depends very largely upon circumstances. The essence of the moral dilemma must be found in the necessity to choose, and yet the inability to justify a choice, between moral claims which, although regarded as equally compelling, have become irreconcilable.[2]

---

for the reason that war involves the taking of measures which bring suffering to the innocent. Nevertheless, the tragic quality attached to the action need not imply a basic uncertainty over taking the action if the values the actor seeks to preserve are thought to outweigh those values that must be sacrificed. The moral dilemma encompasses the tragic situation and goes beyond it in that it implies an inability to justify a choice between political strategies whose consequences are mutually exclusive, yet whose values are equally compelling.

[2] Of course, moral dilemmas in statecraft need never arise if policy is clearly informed by a "higher purpose," a purpose overriding any claims whose observance would detract from or jeopardize that purpose. Thus if the security and power of the nation is taken as the ultimate standard by

It is only natural that men should prove reluctant to acknowledge the possibility of moral dilemmas arising in foreign policy. Still, in view of the prospects held out by nuclear conflict, it surely is not without significance that a preoccupation with the possible justification for invoking nuclear force has been looked upon as a kind of disease. Nor can it be without significance that the policy of nuclear deterrence pursued over the past decade has never provoked

which all action should be judged, the possibility of a "pure" moral dilemma arising in statecraft is precluded. Equally precluded, however, is the possibility that foreign policy will be restrained by principles whose observance might require the sacrifice of this "higher purpose." Nevertheless, Hans J. Morgenthau writes: "A foreign policy that does not permit mass extermination as a means to its end does not impose this limitation upon itself because of considerations of political expediency. On the contrary, expediency would counsel such a thorough and effective operation. The limitation derives from an absolute moral principle which must be obeyed regardless of considerations of national advantage. A foreign policy of this kind, therefore, actually sacrifices the national interest where its consistent pursuit would necessitate the violation of a moral principle, such as the prohibition of mass killings in times of peace . . . the fact of the matter is that nations recognize a moral obligation to refrain from the infliction of death and suffering under certain conditions despite the possibility of justifying such conduct in the light of a higher purpose, such as the national interest." *Politics Among Nations* (2nd ed., 1954), pp. 213-14. Although it is asserted that the "national interest" constitutes the "higher purpose," and that the consistent pursuit of the national interest may necessitate mass extermination, it is nevertheless insisted that such action cannot be taken because of a presumably lower but absolute moral principle. Yet if the latter principle is absolute and prevails over the national interest, it may do so only because it constitutes the higher value. In essence, Professor Morgenthau argues that although the higher purpose is the national interest, defined primarily in terms of the nation's security and power, that purpose may not be achieved by these particular means, that is, the mass extermination of a defeated enemy. But what can this assertion imply save that the avoidance of these means is prescribed by a norm superior to that norm or purpose embodied in the national interest? On the other hand, if the "higher purpose," the superior value, is indeed the national interest, and if the national interest is defined in terms of the nation's security and power, there is no basis—whether expediential or moral—for rejecting a policy of mass extermination provided only that this policy is in fact calculated to achieve its ends.

a crisis of conscience.[3] It is instructive to recall the relative ease with which an extreme version of nuclear deterrence was generally accepted when publicly proclaimed by Secretary of State Dulles in 1954. Apart from a small minority, "massive retaliation" was not a source of moral embarrassment, let alone a source of moral anguish, for a nation which professes to see itself as an expression of a liberal and humanitarian ethic. On the contrary, that policy was regarded as fully consonant with the moral law, although its essential feature lay in the disavowal of any inherent limits to the "defensive" use of nuclear force other than those limits imposed by expediency. Thus if the official expositors of "massive retaliation" acknowledged restraints on the employment of force, it was, as Secretary Dulles pointed out, because "massive atomic and thermonuclear retaliation is not the kind of power which could most usefully be invoked under all circumstances."[4] Since the justification for reliance upon a strategy of nuclear deterrence was taken as self-evident, the problem of implementing that strategy could be reduced to the technical considerations of obtaining "maximum protection at minimum cost."

It is quite true that this nation's response to the prospect of employing force—any kind of force—has exhibited a measure of moral anxiety. Until very recently, however, this anxiety has been largely confined to questioning the circumstances in which force may be resorted to rather than the weapons and methods that may be employed in responding

[3] One eminent scientist, reflecting on this experience, has written: "I find myself profoundly in anguish over the fact that no ethical discourse of any nobility or weight has been addressed to the problem of the atomic weapons. . . . What are we to think of such a civilization, which has not been able to talk about the prospect of killing almost everybody, except in prudential and game-theoretic terms." J. Robert Oppenheimer, "In the Keeping of Unreason," *Bulletin of the Atomic Scientists,* January, 1960, p. 22.

[4] John Foster Dulles, "Policy for Security and Peace," *Foreign Affairs,* xxxii (April, 1954), 356.

to aggression. The strategy of nuclear deterrence has, of course, threatened to lead to crises of confidence whenever its credibility and general effectiveness has been challenged by events. Yet these crises only serve to emphasize the point that the justification for this policy has been taken for granted.

Criticism of the manner in which deterrence has been applied has stemmed almost entirely from prudential considerations. The moral problem in foreign policy is not simply a problem of how to act prudently, however. There can be no moral behavior in statecraft without prudence, that is, without a concern for the consequences of action and a willingness to accept responsibility for those consequences. But prudence surely cannot be the whole, or even the basis of that behavior. Prudence places no restraints on policy other than caution and circumspection; it sets no limits to self-interest other than those limits imposed by the situation in which policy must be conducted; it is compatible with any and all purposes which hold out the prospect of success.[5] Before the statesman can be prudent there must be something for him to be prudent about. To reduce the moral problem in foreign policy to a problem of prudence, to see in moral uncertainty little more than the reflection of political-military uncertainty, is necessarily to assume a

[5] Hitler was imprudent, but an adverse moral judgment of his statecraft need not be based simply on his imprudence. On the other hand, Stalin was prudent, but his prudence need not be regarded as a compelling reason for according moral approval to Stalinist statecraft. The view that sees the moral problem in statecraft as primarily a problem of prudence was expressed by Machiavelli in these terms: "Nor is it to be supposed that a state can ever adopt a course that is entirely safe; on the contrary, a prince must make up his mind to take the chance of all the doubts and uncertainties; for such is the order of things that one inconvenience cannot be avoided except at the risk of being exposed to another. And it is the province of prudence to discriminate amongst these inconveniences, and to accept the least evil for good." *The Prince,* Chap. xxi. Machiavelli assumed that the higher purpose of statecraft was the security and power of the

higher purpose that must guide the statesman and to which
all other purposes must be subordinated. A distinction
should be drawn then between the moral dilemma that
arises from equally compelling though irreconcilable moral
demands and the dilemma that arises from uncertainty over
the consequences of alternative courses of action. Criticisms
of the strategy of nuclear deterrence have been almost invariably concerned with the latter dilemma, that is with the
problem of how to act prudently in an environment that is
sufficiently novel to make prudent behavior very difficult.

The argument has been frequently advanced that deterrence has reflected throughout no more than the instinctive
will to survive that lies at the root of every nation's foreign
policy. In this view, the strategy of nuclear deterrence has
simply been the response that collectives, like individuals,
will invariably make once they consider their survival imperiled. To preserve their liberty and identity they will
instinctively react by threatening to employ any means and
to take any measures in order to fend off the aggressor. The
"justification" for deterrence, then, is presumably that it has
been a "necessary" policy, a "natural" response to a situation
permitting no alternatives. Moral dilemmas can arise, however, only where the possibility of choice exists, not where
the freedom to choose has been foreclosed.

Although the circumstances to which it is applied are
novel enough, the endeavor to justify a policy of deterrence

state. Moral action for the statesman is thereby identified with successful
political action, or perhaps more accurately with the requirements for
successful political action drawn from the environment in which the action
takes place. Hence, an action will be immoral when it does not conform
to the requirements which determine political success, when it is calculated
to result in a reduction of the state's security and power. Conversely, as
long as a policy is calculated to achieve these goals it can—and indeed
must—be morally approved, whatever else may be its consequences. It is
a significant commentary on the history of this view, however, that very
few among its advocates have been willing consistently to accept its consequences.

by equating it with necessity is perhaps as old as statecraft itself. Nothing seems quite so congenial to men as the conviction that what they have chosen to do has in reality not been their choice at all, that they have only acted as they have had to act. Nor can it prove surprising if the enormity of the retaliatory measures to which a strategy of nuclear deterrence has been committed should make this conviction particularly appealing. Yet even if the assumption were to be granted that the behavior of collectives is in fact somehow as predetermined as the "instinctive" behavior of individuals, would this compel the conclusion that the issue of national survival thereby transcends moral judgment? Would not the critical question of the measures a nation may take in attempting to insure its survival still remain one over which the possibility of choice cannot be excluded?

These questions, of course, take for granted a situation in which the issue of national survival is for all practicable purposes unmistakable because the threat is both direct and immediate. Even more, they assume a desperate situation in which survival of the nation can be preserved, if at all, only by pursuing one course of action, though a course of action that will if undertaken lead to consequences of such a nature as to confront men with a terrible dilemma. But the strategy of nuclear deterrence did not spring from such a situation, although it foreshadowed that situation as a future possibility. At any rate, the awareness of a situation in which the issue of national survival may indeed be posed in such clear and desperate terms has come only very gradually over the past decade. If nuclear deterrence is to be equated simply with an instinctive will to survive, then an unease over the moral risks and dilemmas this strategy implied might have been expected to mark the period in which deterrence was initiated and developed. In these earlier years deterrence was evidently not a response to a direct survival threat. Other nations were directly confronted with the prospect of losing their identity. However serious that prospect may have been for American security, it constituted a problem of security and not of survival.[6]

It is at present that the survival argument should prove persuasive and that an instinctive will to survive might be expected to overcome any sense of moral unease or uncertainty over the justification for a strategy of nuclear deterrence. Yet the record appears to indicate a rather different sequence. If anything, a sense of restraint in threatening to employ nuclear weapons and a moral sensitivity over the justification for ever employing these weapons is more apparent today than in an earlier period. A nation that once manifested little concern over the threat to visit an aggressor with nuclear destruction if the latter in resorting to armed force thereby jeopardized its security now shows signs of becoming sensitive to the moral hazards implicit in a strategy of nuclear deterrence. Yet that strategy has now become increasingly synonymous with the issue of survival itself.

No doubt this belated awareness of the moral risks attending a strategy of nuclear deterrence must in part be found in an increasing awareness of the physical risks deterrence

---

[6] Obviously, the distinction between security and survival is seldom easy to draw until perhaps it is too late. But this is hardly sufficient reason for considering the distinction nonexistent or without significance. There are degrees of security, or insecurity, but a nation either survives in the physical sense or it does not survive. To be sure, a nation's prospects for survival over an indefinite period is a function of the degree of security it enjoys. It does not follow, however, that it is therefore impossible to distinguish between the varying prospects for survival and an immediate threat to survival. A decade ago the Soviet threat to this nation was one which could be regarded only in terms of American prospects for survival, not of survival itself. Soviet occupation of any one of a number of areas would have diminished these prospects; Soviet occupation of Western Europe would have diminished these propects very severely. But as long as the Soviets lacked the means to direct a successful strategic nuclear attack against this nation the threat necessarily remained one of security and not of survival.

must now involve. As long as the physical risks incurred were of a wholly different order of magnitude, the moral risks could be regarded with complacency. To be sure, the suggestion that a newly gained scruple over the consequences of employing nuclear weapons is not unrelated to the growing nuclear capability of the adversary is somewhat less than flattering; it implies an insensitivity that is responsive only to the fear of retaliation in kind. Nor is it easily reconciled with the image we find congenial to draw of ourselves as a nation. Yet it would be pointless to deny that a monopoly or decisive superiority in the new weaponry eased the acceptance of a strategy for deterring aggression that acknowledged no inherent restraints on the retaliatory measures which might be taken against an aggressor. It would be equally pointless to deny that a desire to regain a security we once possessed and to regain that security in the most painless and economical manner prompted the acceptance of a strategy that in its extreme version did not hesitate to threaten an aggressor with virtual annihilation.[7]

II

It is necessary to emphasize the extent to which the strategy of deterrence was shaped, whether consciously or unconsciously, by considerations of self-interest and expediency, as well as to insist upon the degree to which "con-

[7] The predominant form deterrence took in the 1950's may be seen not only as the reflection of a deep-rooted desire to regain a security we had once possessed, or at least thought we possessed, but to regain that security through methods we had once successfully employed. In effect, this strategy has implied either no military involvement—save for "brushfires," etc.—or massive involvement that would be quickly and decisively waged. In either case, the agonizing and indecisive kind of military involvement symbolized by Korea would be avoided. It is clear that these alternatives were very close to the alternatives presupposed by traditional policy, a policy abandoned on the political though not on the military level.

venience" rather than "necessity" determined the character of that strategy. At the same time, a strategy of nuclear deterrence could not have been accepted with the ease it was had it not been given a justification that transcended considerations of self-interest and expediency.[8] Nor could deterrence have been so readily accepted had it not been informed by the expectation that it would serve as an instrument for banishing force altogether from history. Indeed, though the circumstances in which deterrence must now operate have profoundly changed, the essential justification for this strategy has throughout remained unchanged. Even more significant, perhaps, in view of this altered environment, has been a reluctance to alter the expectations that informed deterrence in an earlier period.

The central moral issue that the strategy of nuclear deterrence has always raised can be simply put: what are the limits to the measures a nation may threaten to take in responding to the aggressive use of force? Although we have assumed that the essential justification for a deterrent

---

[8] On the other hand, Leo Szilard concludes that the acceptance of a policy threatening "massive retaliation," despite its obvious moral risks, "just goes to show that—contrary to what many Americans would like to believe—the American government, much like the governments of all the other great powers, is guided on all really vital issues by considerations of expediency rather than by moral considerations." "How to Live with the Bomb—and Survive," *Bulletin of the Atomic Scientists,* February, 1960, p. 62. This conclusion is doubly misleading in that it exaggerates both the cynicism of governments and the innocence of the governed. The American people were not wholly oblivious to the moral hazards of threatening massive retaliation, nor were they entirely unaware of the extent to which this policy was prompted by considerations of expediency. They endorsed this policy nonetheless. The American government was not guided simply by considerations of expediency. There is no reason to question the sincerity of those officials who insisted throughout that massive retaliation was a purely defensive policy, that it was designed to protect the legitimate interests of others as much as it was designed to preserve our own interests, and that the risks thereby assumed were not out of proportion to the good sought. The validity of these claims is, of course, another matter.

strategy must be found in its obviously defensive purpose, we have also tended to assume that there really are no inherent limits to the measures a nation may thus threaten and, should the need ever arise, take. What is necessary is only that such measures have a defensive character, and they will have a defensive character as long as they have an essentially defensive purpose. The moral purity of a strategy of deterrence has therefore been equated with the purity of its defensive purpose. However, not only does this purpose not impose limits on the measures that may be threatened in order to discourage potential aggressors, but its logic is to resist any attempt to set limits to the deterrent threat since the acknowledgment of substantive limits may well have the consequence of impairing the effectiveness of the threat and hence diluting the purity of its defensive purpose.[9] A potential aggressor may, of course, be deterred from resorting to aggression if he is reasonably certain that his aims will be frustrated, though no more than frustrated. He will simply be denied the fruits of aggression and the *status quo ante bellum* will be restored. But a would-be aggressor is even more likely to be deterred from aggression, this argument insists, if he is reasonably certain that he will be punished, that he will be deprived of something he values, as a consequence of attempting aggression. And if this is true, it follows that he is still more likely to be deterred if he has reason to believe that he may be punished very severely.

[9] It is this logic which perhaps explains the apparent contradiction between an insistence upon making the "punishment fit the crime" and a refusal to elaborate on the nature and limits of the punishment. It is the same reasoning that explains the apparent contradiction between an insistence that aggressors go to war because they "miscalculate," and a reluctance to allow aggressors to calculate save in the most general terms. To make the "punishment fit the crime," to allow aggressors to "calculate" the risks they run in resorting to aggression, implies the setting of reasonably clear limits to the measures peace-loving nations will take in responding to aggression. But this is bad, since it may impair the effectiveness of the deterrent threat.

To be sure, it does not follow that the measures threatened by this particular version of a deterrent strategy are always and necessarily without limit. If a would-be aggressor can indeed be effectively inhibited by a deterrent threat that bears a distinctly limited character, there is no basis—moral or otherwise—for confronting him with a still greater threat. Yet once this reasoning is accepted, it does follow that the character of the deterrent threat is not primarily determined either by the character of the possible aggression or by any consideration of the inherent limits on the employment of force that must be observed even in a defensive war. Instead, the character of the deterrent threat will be determined by the desire to achieve the greatest possible certainty in preventing the resort—any resort—to aggression.

Once this desire becomes the paramount objective of a deterrent strategy, once such a strategy is informed by the desire and expectation of banishing aggressive force altogether from history, there remain no limits to the measures aggressors may be threatened with save perhaps those limits that are imposed by considerations of prudence. It is, therefore, the certainty attached to the deterrent threat rather than the precise nature of the threat that must form the primary object of concern. Of course, the degree of certainty that may be attached to the deterrent threat is in part a function of its nature, in the sense that it simply may not be reasonable in certain circumstances to expect a would-be aggressor to believe that the measures threatened would in fact be carried out. But from this point of view the credibility of the deterrent threat is solely a technical problem governed by the underlying assumption that what can be made credible to the adversary is *per se* good. And it is for this reason that the critical controversies over deterrence have centered mainly on the question: what are the limits of credibility a deterrent strategy must observe? Those limits have been described by political-military calculations and by "psychological" considerations, but they have not been described by restraints that transcend prudence or expediency.

It has already been suggested that if the strategy of deterrence is considered from the point of view of its possible "failure" rather than from the expectation of "success" if the measures threatened must ever be carried out, the character of the measures taken promises to be more than defensive. It is true that deterrence has always been justified by the argument that these measures would of necessity have a defensive character since they would be taken for a defensive purpose, that is, for the purpose of resisting aggression. But this argument only serves to obscure the very issue requiring examination. It begs the decisive question, for it regards as defensive those measures that by almost any reasonable standard are surely more than defensive in their effects. If it is once accepted, the literal annihilation of an aggressor may readily be justified as a defensive measure. All that is necessary is that the act of annihilation be attended by a defensive purpose!

In part, the insistence upon regarding as defensive those measures that may encompass even the annihilation of a potential aggressor stems from an obsession intent upon identifying the character of war, and consequently the measures taken in war, with the circumstances attending war's origin. In part, however, this insistence stems from an equation of the purposes sought by the deterrent threat with the actual consequences of this threat if it should ever prove necessary to carry it out. But the purposes sought by the deterrent threat, *qua* threat, cannot simply be equated with the consequences of carrying out that threat; there is no reason to assume that the purposes informing the threat necessarily mark as well the consequences that may follow if the threat should ever be carried out. The purposes sought by the threat may indeed be entirely defensive. At the same time, the consequences attending the carrying out of this purely defensive threat may well be more than defensive. In a word, the character of the threat must be considered quite independent of the character of the measures that are threatened; the defensive purpose of the former does not insure the defensive character of the latter.

The reasons for this conclusion are clear enough. Whether or not a war may be characterized as defensive is not dependent simply upon the circumstances that mark its initiation. Nor is its defensive character necessarily evidenced by the reluctance with which a nation resorts to force in response to armed aggression. There is nothing that prevents an aversion to force from giving rise, once at war, to the determination that force should be employed to the end that war may be banished altogether from history. The measures required for the realization of so far-reaching a purpose as this may prove equally far-reaching; experience has demonstrated that they may easily result in consequences which represent a radical change in the *status quo ante bellum*. If the argument is once accepted that these measures nevertheless have a purely defensive character, presumably because they are taken for what is held to be no more than a defensive purpose, then there is very little that cannot be reconciled with an allegedly defensive war. But the character of a war surely cannot be determined simply by its professed purposes, however great the sincerity with which those purposes may be held. The character of a war must instead be determined primarily by the consequences to which it may ultimately lead, consequences that will result from the measures taken in waging war, consequences that will follow from the manner in which the war is conducted. There is still greater reason to insist that the character of a war must be determined by the nature of the measures a nation threatens to employ against potential aggressors and intends to employ should would-be aggressors ever miscalculate.

These considerations evoke an age-old paradox that may now be pushed to an extreme, given the potentialities of the new technology. Once the purity of the defensive purpose sought by a strategy of deterrence is measured by the effectiveness of the deterrent threat, such a strategy becomes marked with a profoundly ambivalent character. For the more "purely defensive" the purpose sought by the deterrent threat, the less defensive the consequences promise to be should that strategy ever "fail." In this manner, an altogether legitimate desire for security against aggression may nonetheless give rise to a strategy of deterring potential aggressors by the threat of measures which if ever acted upon must prove far more than defensive. When carried to an extreme, a purely defensive purpose is readily translated into a threat to take measures that may well entail the utter annihilation of potential aggressors.

It is this paradox that illuminates the central moral question raised by a strategy of deterrence. In an uncertain and unpredictable world what are the limits to the measures with which aggressors ought to be threatened? This question cannot be turned aside by the response that since a strategy of deterrence has a defensive purpose the measures which form the deterrent threat may be left solely to expediential or prudential considerations. Even if it were to be assumed that the measures with which an aggressor is threatened necessarily retain a purely defensive character should the need ever arise to carry them out, this distinctly moral problem would still remain. In view of the moral hazards that must inevitably attend the employment of force, what is the justification for employing more force than is absolutely necessary for the immediate task of defending those interests directly imperiled by aggression, a task which is itself—as a preceding essay has sought to demonstrate—never free from a certain degree of ambiguity? And if the justification for going beyond these narrowly conceived bounds of a defensive war is always difficult to establish, what is the justification for threatening to employ measures that have no discernible limits? In particular, what is the justification for threatening to employ such measures in circumstances where the requirements of defense, though no more than the strictly conceived requirements of defense, may be satisfied by a distinctly limited form of deterrent threat?

It will, of course, be said that to exorcise aggression, or, at the very least, to reduce the possibility of aggression to negligible proportions, is precisely the kind of purpose that may justify even the most extreme form of deterrent. Clearly, the strategy of nuclear deterrence has been informed throughout by the expectation that a threat of sufficient magnitude, made with apparent determination, would provide the means to the realization of this purpose. In turn, the expectation that aggressive force may thus be banished from history has furnished the principal justification for deterrence, and particularly for its more extreme versions. If the measures that might be taken should deterrence fail have been further justified as being no more than strictly defensive in character, this justification has nevertheless remained subordinate to the theme that deterrence would not fail. To be sure, the consequences following upon the "failure" of deterrence in an earlier period could yet be regarded with relative equanimity. Still, the moral complacency with which the strategy of nuclear deterrence was initially accepted cannot be attributed simply to a confidence that the adversary was unable to retaliate in kind. Nor can this complacency be attributed simply to the strength of a doctrine intent upon characterizing any measures taken in response to "aggression" as purely "defensive."

However significant these factors may have been, the principal moral criticism that could be made of a strategy of nuclear deterrence was always readily apparent and consisted in the marked disparity intended between the evil to be deterred and the means with which evil-doers were to be punished if they nevertheless refused to be deterred. But the complacency with which this criticism was met cannot be laid simply to a callousness to the consequences attendant upon a failure of deterrence. If a strategy of threatening would-be aggressors with severe punishment was not considered to impose grave moral risks, the reason must largely be found in the sanguine conviction that this strategy would doubtless succeed. Given the remarkable strength of this conviction, it is understandable that the moral criticism seemed without substance since it appeared to miss the central feature of this strategy. A concern over the justification for ever taking the measures threatened by a strategy of nuclear deterrence necessarily assumed that this strategy might "fail." But the essential claim of deterrence has always been that the contingency feared would never arise if only the threat were to be made with the requisite determination.

Does this description exaggerate the expectations of deterrence? It may so appear if the claims that have been made on behalf of deterrence are taken literally. Certainly, the most articulate spokesmen for the strategy of nuclear deterrence have never contended that this strategy would provide an absolute guarantee against any further resort to aggression; they have not insisted that deterrence would inhibit any and all "crimes of violence" in the international society. Instead, deterrence has been generally described as "reducing the likelihood of aggression," as creating the "probability" that potential aggressors would refrain from carrying out their designs for conquest. The principle of deterrence, Secretary Dulles averred on several occasions, "does not operate one hundred percent even in the best ordered communities." Why should any better performance be expected when this principle is applied to the society of nations?

Nevertheless, if the qualifications that have admittedly marked the exposition of the strategy of deterrence are taken literally, then the justification for this strategy can hardly be taken seriously. Within domestic societies the principle of deterrence need not be one hundred per cent effective to prove its value. Moreover, the consequences following a failure of deterrence are not catastrophic for the community as a whole. Here, the principle of deterrence is quite compatible with a limited number of "failures" precisely because these failures, and the subsequent measures of repression taken against individual lawbreakers, do not threaten the well-being of the entire community. On the other hand, the repression of the national lawbreaker obviously does threaten the well-being of the greater society of nations, or at least a substantial portion of it. Given the consequences of "nuclear punishment," the political and moral justification of nuclear deterrence cannot rest on the mere claim that deterrence reduces the number of "crimes of violence," since the absurdity of this claim is patent. Here, the principle of deterrence is evidently not compatible with a number of "failures," however limited that number, if any one of these failures may eventuate in a general nuclear conflict.

There is a profound difference then in the meaning that must be, and has been, imputed to the principle of deterrence in contemporary American strategy. It consists in the perfectionist expectations attached to the operation of this principle. For it is only by harboring such expectations that deterrence can find a seemingly plausible justification. This justification, and the expectations on which it rests, may prove quite compatible, however, with the admission of "brushfires" and other very minor outbreaks of violence. The latter need not be interpreted as representing failures of deterrence. Nor need they be seen as really incompatible with the goal of banishing force from history. Indeed, it is the very occurrence of these minor outbreaks that may serve to confirm, rather than to detract from, the central expectations aroused by a deterrent strategy. "Brushfires" may give a semblance of reality to deterrence that would otherwise be lacking, in appearing to demonstrate that deterrence does not and need not "operate one hundred per cent." But since "brushfires" are not wars, the principal expectations of deterrence, and consequently the principal justification given that strategy, may nevertheless remain essentially unimpaired.

III

An earlier essay suggested that the American just war doctrine cannot be seen simply as the product of "pure" moral conviction. This doctrine is also the result of a particular historic experience, an experience that gave rise to a markedly voluntaristic interpretation of conflict. The fervor with which we have condemned the deliberate recourse to war as an instrument of national policy reflects more than a moral aversion to the methods of violence. It also stems from a belief that nations "need" never resort to force. War is not only an evil, it is a wholly unnecessary evil.

In this view, there is nothing that impels nations to use force, no conflicts of interest so intractable that force will appear as the only solution, no deep-rooted insecurity that can seemingly find an outlet only in aggression. Neither is it possible to regard aggression as somehow a function of the very nature of international society. On the contrary, when nations resort to force, they choose a course of action they might readily have avoided. Aggression, therefore, is the result of deliberate evil wedded to accident, the accident of miscalculation. When aggressive governments resort to force they have concluded that their evil designs will succeed and

are convinced that they can "get away with it," because
other nations through excessive trust or neglect or irresolu-
tion have encouraged them in this belief. It follows that
peace is above all dependent upon insuring that would-be
aggressors are never given the opportunity to miscalculate;
they must be persuaded that the risks undertaken in resorting to aggression outweigh the gains they hope to achieve.
The strategy of peace-loving nations must consist in a willingness to accept this task of persuasion with the requisite will
and determination.

The strategy of nuclear deterrence obviously did not
spring full-blown from these convictions alone. Yet it is
clear that these convictions significantly eased the acceptance
of this strategy and nourished the extraordinary expectations that deterrence called forth. In an earlier period, the
faith manifested in nuclear deterrence might be explained
by the confidence placed in this nation's monopoly or preponderant strength in nuclear weapons. Aggressors then
could not reasonably doubt our determination to make
aggression costly by imposing on them risks out of all proportion to the possible gains they might expect from resorting to aggression. But this faith in an ever-triumphant will
is bound to be difficult to sustain once the aggressor possesses the means to answer any threat by the counterthreat
of retaliation in kind. If the faith initially elicited by a
strategy of nuclear deterrence nevertheless persists in radically changed circumstances, the explanation must in part
be found in the conviction that aggressors may be readily
deterred precisely because they have no real need to resort
to force. This being so, the ends of aggression can rarely,
if indeed ever, appear so important to an aggressor as to
justify the risks that attempting to obtain them by force
might impose. The same conviction must serve to encourage
the assumption that the risks run in applying a strategy of
nuclear deterrence are not likely to prove high, since the

risks of the deterrer are no more than a function of the needs of the nation to be deterred.

Experience may confound dogma, however, and afford examples of very determined aggressors. If a strategy of nuclear deterrence is to succeed in exorcising aggression, in every contest of wills the will of peace-loving nations must always prove stronger in the end than the will of the aggressor. From the start the psychology behind the strategy of nuclear deterrence has assumed that this requirement of an ever-triumphant will could be satisfied, if only because strength of will must somehow be proportionate to nobility of purpose. If our heart is pure, our hand will be steady, or at least steadier than the aggressor's. If our purposes are superior to those of the adversary, if they represent right and justice, then it must follow that our determination to defend those purposes will prove stronger—and this quite apart from the concrete circumstances that may attend a test of wills.

At the same time, if our will is to prove triumphant whenever and wherever it is tested by the aggressor, it can do so only if each test of wills, each issue, is identified with our vital interests as a nation and with our over-all purposes in the world. Nothing could be more fatal to the success of a strategy of nuclear deterrence than attempting to isolate the immediate issue in dispute, thereby separating it from the larger issues to which it is related or for which it must serve as an essential symbol. For if the specific interest threatened by aggression is once considered in isolation from the vital interests and overarching purposes of which it forms an integral part, the risks may well appear so great that the justification for invoking the deterrent threat may be seriously questioned. The inevitable consequence, it is argued, will be a corrosion of will and the encouragement of the aggressor.

Thus if the islands of Quemoy and Matsu, or even Formosa, are threatened by Chinese Communist aggression, the will to deter aggression must prove difficult to maintain unless the threat is also seen as a critical challenge to the principle that territorial disputes shall not be settled by the instrument of force. Upon the observance of that vital principle the hope for international order must ultimately rest. "No country should use armed force to seize new territory," Secretary Dulles declared in September 1958, responding to a Chinese Communist threat to seize the offshore islands of Quemoy and Matsu. To those who doubted whether the specific issue in dispute justified the risks that were run in deterring a Communist assault by the threat of nuclear retaliation, Mr. Dulles responded by calling attention to the vital importance of restraining those who would "defy the basic principle upon which world order depends, namely, that armed force should not be used to achieve territorial ambitions. . . . Acquiescence therein [to Communist threats] would threaten peace everywhere." [10]

Again, if the independence of West Berlin is threatened by Soviet demands which, once granted, might lead to that city's absorption by the adversary, the issue cannot be seen simply as one involving the freedom of a city. Could the interest in preserving the freedom of a city, any city, justify the risks that might be entailed by invoking a strategy of nuclear deterrence? Berlin cannot be regarded merely as a city; it must be seen as a symbol of freedom to those in the East who remain enslaved by the Soviet tyranny. Even more important, Berlin must be seen as the essential symbol of the West's determination to resist further Soviet encroachment. The weakening of that symbol would herald the disintegration of the Western alliance and thereby eventually put an end to the political independence of Western Europe. An end to the independence of Western Europe

[10] Statement to Press, September 4, 1958 (*Bulletin*, xxxix, 446).

would in turn signal a decisive shift in the world balance of power, a shift that would leave this nation isolated and increasingly subject to Soviet blandishments. What is at stake, then, in a contest of wills over Berlin is not the security and independence of a city but the very survival of the Free World.[11]

These examples could be multiplied. The point they are intended to illustrate, however, is not that the reasoning they suggest is somehow unique to the strategy of nuclear deterrence nor that this reasoning is necessarily unfounded. In some sense, it is perfectly true that the forcible seizure of the islands of Quemoy and Matsu would weaken the principle that territorial disputes shall not be resolved by the instrument of force. In some sense, it is abundantly clear that what is at stake in the continuing dispute over the status of West Berlin is not only the security and independence of a city but the prospects for survival of the Free World. Yet the relevant point is not the degree to which these claims may be valid but the compulsion that operates to make them as absolute as possible. If the will to deter aggression depends on the conviction that the purposes served by deterrence justify beyond doubt the risks incurred

[11] "No issue on earth today is more critical," the Under Secretary of State declared in a review of the American position on Berlin. "It bears directly upon the future stability of Central Europe and the possibility of a lasting European peace. It represents a critical test of the integrity and dependability of the free world's collective security systems, because no nation could preserve its faith in collective security if we permitted the courageous people of West Berlin to be sold into slavery." Address by Douglas Dillon to American Federation of Labor-Congress of Industrial Organizations Conference on World Affairs, New York, April 20, 1960 (*Bulletin,* xlii, 724). With these interests at stake, the conclusion to be drawn is plain. The present integrity of Berlin must be preserved at any price, even if that price must include a willingness to threaten nuclear conflict. To be sure, it may be rather difficult, as President Eisenhower has observed, to see how the employment of nuclear weapons could preserve Berlin's integrity. But this difficulty may presumably be overcome if only the necessary will to invoke the nuclear deterrent is maintained.

in invoking this strategy, the purposes must of necessity always appear very great indeed. Without this conviction a strategy of nuclear deterrence may readily be deprived both of its political and of its moral justification. Without this conviction the will to invoke the nuclear deterrent with the requisite degree of determination would certainly corrode.

These considerations suggest that the strategy of nuclear deterrence has its deepest roots in what might well be termed an act of faith. As such, that strategy must in the final analysis prove independent of prudential calculation and rational considerations. The "higher rationality" of deterrence might therefore be formulated in the following manner: It is not prudence but faith in ourselves and in our purposes that is ultimately needed to achieve the goal of banishing aggressive force from history. To persuade the would-be aggressor we need only first persuade ourselves. To convince the adversary that we would act in the manner threatened, it is indispensable to convince ourselves that we would so respond. As long as we believe, others will believe. And as long as others believe, they will not act. The key to a successful strategy of nuclear deterrence lies wholly within ourselves.

IV

The principal difficulty of the strategy of nuclear deterrence has always been that, like all faiths, not everyone will believe it. Those at whom it is directed may nevertheless remain incredulous, if only because they are expected to conform to a pattern of behavior from which the true believers are somehow exempt. If aggressors are never to miscalculate, they must be persuaded that the risks of aggression will always clearly outweigh the possible gains. But this presupposes a world in which the ends sought in the deterrence of aggression will always clearly justify the possible risks. History must therefore be expected to demonstrate not one but two laws governing human conduct, the one applicable to aggressor nations and the other applicable to peace-loving nations. Nor is this all. Deterrence must convert by persuading unbelievers that a will exists to use the sword. Yet nuclear deterrence is a faith whose justification rests upon the claim to convert through persuasion alone and not by the sword. Unlike other faiths, though, the peculiar characteristic, and weakness, of deterrence is that it cannot afford disbelief. The actual use of the sword testifies not only to disbelief but also to a profound "failure" of that faith. What is far worse, the consequences that must be expected to attend a failure of faith, though the threat of these consequences forms a legitimate part of the process of conversion, can find no clear justification. If anything, the consequences that are expected to attend a failure to convert must stand condemned.

There is admittedly no logical reason for concluding that this faith cannot succeed. If a strategy of nuclear deterrence may succeed in preventing a direct assault upon this nation, the possibility cannot be excluded that the same strategy may be effectively extended to deter armed aggression against other nations as well. But a criticism of deterrence need not depend upon establishing that this strategy cannot succeed; it need only demonstrate the existence of a substantial possibility that it may fail and that failure would in all likelihood lead to the consequences promised by the deterrent threat. Unlike other defensive strategies, nuclear deterrence cannot find a justification simply by demonstrating a probability of success. Given the consequences of "failure" and the inability to provide a satisfactory justification for these consequences, a strategy of nuclear deterrence must demonstrate instead that its prospects for success approach the point of near certainty. Yet the possibility of providing such a demonstration is denied both by logic and by experience.

It is precisely this requirement, and the inherent impossibility of its satisfaction, that involves a deterrent strategy in a moral paradox, particularly when it must be applied against an adversary able to retaliate in kind. A deterrent strategy that is genuinely motivated in some measure by a concern for the security of other nations will seek to extend the area to which it will be applied. Yet to the degree that nuclear deterrence is extended to others it must fall increasingly short of the requirement that it achieve an effectiveness bordering on certainty. However sincere the desire to transcend self-interest, the endeavor to realize this desire in the form of a strategy of nuclear deterrence must inevitably stimulate the incredulity of an opponent who, as we have ourselves so frequently insisted, interprets our behavior as the manifestation of unalloyed self-interest. If a willingness to extend a deterrent strategy to others does in fact reflect a genuine concern for others, it is nevertheless a concern that in the present circumstances cannot but invite miscalculation by a would-be aggressor. No doubt it is both unnecessary and perverse to insist that a danger of miscalculation must thereby condemn this concern. But it is surely not perverse to suggest that a danger of miscalculation may condemn the strategy that has formed the concrete expression of this concern.

What if the faith in a strategy of nuclear deterrence could somehow be vindicated beyond all doubt, however, and vindicated in a manner that would exceed even the aspirations of the most ardent believers? What if it is assumed that a deterrent strategy can with complete safety, as long as we maintain the requisite will, deter attack upon ourselves and upon others as well, that with the possible exception of "brushfires" and other like outbreaks of a negligible character this strategy can effectively banish force from history?

We may even go further and make the very extravagant assumption that a deterrent strategy can be effectively employed to prevent measures which, though falling short of overt armed aggression, may nevertheless prove almost as inimical in the long run to our concept of a desirable international order, e.g., so-called indirect aggression. We may assume, in other words, that a deterrent faith has not only succeeded in "converting" our opponents, by persuading them that the deterrent threat is wholly credible, but that it has done so beyond our wildest expectations. This is, to be sure, a dream world that we are assuming. Even so, were it realizable, would it of necessity be a desirable world? In this dream world of "maximum credibility" would it still be possible to doubt the justification for a strategy of nuclear deterrence? What would be the probable nature of the international society to which this dream world would give rise? Would it be a society in which we might realize our purposes as a nation? Or would it be a society that would serve instead to frustrate and eventually even to corrupt those purposes?

It is first of all clear that we cannot assume an international society in which our adversaries would somehow be reconciled to us. At the very least, we clearly have no right to make this assumption either for the present or for the immediately foreseeable future. Quite to the contrary, all that we are justified in assuming is a world in which all forms of aggression—that is, all forms of behavior we may elect to regard as aggression—would be banished because our will is triumphant. But the triumph of our will is evidently not synonymous with a society that finds would-be aggressors reconciled to the given order of things. It can only be a world in which our will is in fact triumphant, and consequently we must accept for the time being an international society that is based not upon consent but on coercion, and indeed on the purest coercion at that.

To be sure, we may nevertheless insist that although the

international society of this dream world is one based on coercion it would eventually give way to a world based on consent. Coercion would presumably yield in time to consent because of the intrinsic justice of the purposes for which coercion would be exercised, purposes whose merit our adversaries of today would eventually acknowledge. Yet even in the dream world we have assumed, the presumption of eventual consent could not detract from the fact that for the time being at least it would not be consent, nor even a partial consent, but the purest form of coercion that would provide the necessary foundation.

The immediate prospect, then, is a world in which the actuality of force has been exorcised, though not a world in which force as such has ceased to play a decisive role. The overt employment of force would be banished from history, but the role of force in history surely would not be reduced to negligible proportions. If anything, we must have reason to expect that force would have a greater importance than ever before, that the threat of force—potential force—would dominate history to a degree that exceeds the bounds of previous experience. In this dream world we should assuredly have peace, in the literal sense that armed force would not be employed. This peace would nevertheless rest upon force, and it would rest upon force to an extent perhaps greater than any peace history has known.

Whether or not the likely consequences of a world of absolute deterrence are approved, they cannot be turned away either by charming though irrelevant metaphors or by appealing though false analogies. The enforcement of peace would be directed, as indeed it is directed today, against vast national communities which make up a significant portion of the human race. We might continue to regard the task of peace enforcement as one of repressing "criminals" and "lawless elements" within the greater society of nations, but this description could not alter the reality of things, not even the reality with which we must endow a dream world of absolutely effective deterrence.

If an analogy must be drawn at all in this respect between domestic and international societies, the parallel situation within domestic society is that of a disaffected group which nevertheless comprises a very substantial portion of the population. Furthermore, though posing the most serious kind of threat to the established order of society and to the values reflected by that order, this group cannot be pictured as made up either of moral idiots who are incapable of comprehending the moral law or of moral cynics who know of no law save their own unbounded will to power. However dangerous the threat posed to the existing order of society, that threat will nevertheless be made in the name of an alternative set of values, sincerely held. Indeed, it may well be the "sincerity" with which these values are held that itself constitutes the critical danger and inhibits any will to compromise, since sincerity here may be but a synonym for a fanaticism that if once given sufficient opportunity might lead the faithful to impose their dogma, if necessary, by force. Peace and the existing order are maintained, however, primarily by threatening this group with annihilation should they once seek to realize their subversive ends through force, whether employed openly or covertly. And since we have assumed in drawing this parallel that the threat is wholly effective, the disaffected group is inhibited not only from employing force in the pursuit of its purposes but even from effectively threatening to employ force.

Whether history furnishes any examples of societies that have in fact reacted in precisely this manner toward subversive groups, and effectively so, is not really in question here. Yet it is surely relevant to ask what price a society might have to pay for success and what consequences might be expected to follow from success. For these are the questions that must be considered in assuming that a strategy of nuclear deterrence might be made absolutely effective not only in preventing a direct attack upon ourselves but particularly in preventing "aggression," both direct and indirect, against others as well. This dream world of an absolutely effective deterrent strategy would insure peace. Would it insure justice as well? Would the peace of deterrence also be a peace with justice? Of course, we have insisted that it would be precisely this, that the only peace we aspire to is a just peace, and that peace and justice are to us but two sides of the same coin. But how can we be so sure that once we are free from the threat of force, a threat that is meaningful because it may always be converted into an actuality, we would listen to the grievances of our adversaries? How can we be so sure that, no longer compelled to consider the demands for change our adversaries might make, we would nevertheless remain at all receptive to these demands, that we would continue to act with moderation and thus merit the praise of those who, as Thucydides described the claim of the Athenians, "nevertheless pay more attention to justice than they are compelled to do by their situation."

If the reply is made that we would remain receptive to demands for change whenever such demands did not violate the minimal requirements of justice, we are nevertheless assuming that we would retain the power to determine the nature of these requirements and whether or not they were met in a concrete situation. But if the history of man's collective relations is to prove of any utility in these matters, it must warn us that we would either not listen at all to the grievances of our adversaries or that at best we would listen only with "one ear." Indeed, does not our own recent experience at least suggest that this is the manner in which we might be expected to react? Yet in spite of the testimony of the past, remote and recent, we are expected to assume that we would somehow manage to defy history and would do so in circumstances holding out an almost unparalleled temptation to the promptings of self-interest.

If this assumption appears unreasonable, it is no less so than the assumption that the dream world of absolutely effective deterrence could be maintained by a political leadership marked by humility and a disposition to compromise with the adversary. Who might be expected to administer this world in which our will remained ever-triumphant? Surely not those who might harbor any doubt about the nobility of our purposes as an expression of the moral law or the justice of the restrictions we had imposed on our adversaries. In logic, there may be no necessity that an absolutely effective deterrent strategy be informed by a faith which leaves no room for doubt about the purity of the wisdom that directs our power. But what may not form a logical requirement may nonetheless form a psychological requirement, men being constituted as they are. If a threat of annihilation is to prove wholly effective, it must be made by a will that permits of no doubt over the justification for ever making this threat. An absolute power to destroy cannot—at least, cannot for long—be effectively threatened without a will endowed with the conviction that the purposes for which this power is threatened are as absolute as the power invoked on their behalf. Nor will it prove sufficient in this situation simply to profess a faith that, while giving an ultimate meaning to human existence, nevertheless is not directly related on every occasion to the relativities which mark the political act. On the contrary, the expectation must be that policy would have to be invested in each instance with an ultimate meaning, else the justification for the act might seem wanting. A justification that appeared less than absolute might corrode the will which must have insured that the deterrent threat was rendered absolutely effective.

Thus the policy required for this dream world would demand much more than a faith which reflected an awareness of the gulf separating it from the moral ambiguities of statecraft. Instead, the effective implementation of policy over a prolonged period of time would almost surely necessitate a fanatical insistence upon identifying the requirements of effective policy with the ultimate imperatives of faith. Is it too much to suggest that those who would possess the qualities necessary to administer such a policy might not possess the qualities of political leadership we have come to regard as desirable for a democratic society?

What we have somehow failed to realize is that in the world as we find it the actuality of force could be banished from history only at a price that we ourselves would be unwilling to pay. What we have somehow failed to appreciate is that the conditions required for realizing the dream world of an absolutely effective strategy of deterrence as well as the likely consequences of this dream world would frustrate rather than fulfill the purposes we have professed as a nation. It is not merely, then, that the expectations aroused by the strategy of nuclear deterrence cannot in practice be realized, but that even if they could, the unqualified success of that strategy would in all likelihood corrupt the purposes it was allegedly designed to serve. The actuality of force would be exorcised but force would nevertheless continue to play a decisive role and perhaps even a greater role than ever before. Instead of a society of consent the immediate expectation must be a society that rested on the ever-present threat of annihilation. The hope that this society would in time be transformed into something other than a relationship founded on pure coercion, that today's repression would nevertheless lead to tomorrow's reconciliation, cannot simply be dismissed out of hand. Yet it is surely a very slender reed on which to rely, since it must assume that men would compromise with their adversaries when there was no longer any need to compromise, and that they would do so even while they remained utterly persuaded that their course represented the path of righteousness for the world.

These considerations, it will be recalled, have assumed the limiting case and are relevant only in criticizing a strategy of nuclear deterrence informed by perfectionist expectations. They are clearly not relevant to a deterrent strategy that is distinctly limited in its aspirations and consequently in what it intends to deter by the threat of massive nuclear retaliation. Such a threat must, in any event, raise insoluble moral dilemmas. Nevertheless, there is a significant difference, both politically and morally, between a deterrent strategy that only employs this threat to prevent potential aggressors from initiating nuclear attack and a deterrent strategy that attempts to employ this threat to the end of exorcising aggression generally. The difference does not stem simply from an increased possibility that a deterrent strategy informed by perfectionist expectations may fail. And it cannot be overcome by the expectation that the measures threatened would never have to be carried out. Even if that expectation is granted, a perfectionist version of deterrence must still represent a strategy imposing exorbitant moral risks precisely because its effective implementation would necessarily involve a claim to what is essentially a monopoly of force, yet a monopoly of force to be exercised over a society that is deeply divided.

It is quite true we have insisted that an effective order of deterrence, effective because our will would be ever-triumphant, must inevitably give rise eventually to a society of consent, not of coercion. Our insistence has rested on the assumption that our purposes in the world are humanity's purposes as well. The order established by deterrence would be transient and provisional since its primary function would be to secure time for the common purposes of humanity to triumph. But if this assumption of a latent con-

sensus awaiting only opportunity to be realized is once
questioned, and it surely must be questioned, the moral
hazards of the force monopoly established though a strategy
of nuclear deterrence are apparent.

V

When we have not sought to ignore the moral dilemmas
raised by a strategy of nuclear deterrence, we have instead
endeavored to persuade ourselves that these dilemmas are not
of our doing. If acknowledged at all, they are nevertheless
held to be a consequence of the new technology and, of
course, the aggressive threats posed by our adversaries.

It would be foolish to accept these protestations of innocence entirely at face value. If we are increasingly confronted with impossible choices between unacceptable evils,
our predicament must in some part be attributed to failures
of our own choosing, to vain expectations that force might
be banished from history, and to an insensitivity over the
means we have been willing to threaten in order to achieve
this end. Our insensitivity has in turn reflected the depth
of conviction in the purity and self-evident character of the
purposes on whose behalf nuclear force has been threatened.
It is this conviction that has frequently led to an unwillingness, perhaps even an inability, to acknowledge the moral
ambiguities that have marked the strategy of nuclear
deterrence.

Nevertheless, an insistence upon recognizing these failures
of our own choosing may easily be carried too far if taken
to suggest that the dilemmas presently incurred by the prospect of employing force might otherwise have been avoided.
Technology is introduced into a political environment which
cannot be transformed suddenly and at will. Unavoidably,
the consequences of technological innovation must be as-

sessed in relation to men's known propensities. To acknowledge this is not to give oneself over to a view that would absolve men of responsibility for the manner in which they employ the instruments provided by technology. It is only to recognize that once a new means of destruction has been developed men's relationships are no longer the same as before. These relationships are no longer the same, not because the new means of destruction will be used, but because they may be used; not because if used they will be used with abandon, but because if used they may be used with abandon.

If it seems too extreme to insist that technology literally imposes moral dilemmas on men, it does not appear excessive to conclude that technology may render irreconcilable moral demands men had previously been able somehow to reconcile. Technology cannot make men bad, but it may surely give rise to circumstances in which it is increasingly difficult to be good. The restraint and moderation men practice are not unrelated to the anxieties they experience, anxieties they have not conjured up from tortured imaginations but which result from an awareness of the harm others may in fact inflict on them. In this sense at least, technology invariably limits the alternatives men will consider and restricts the choices they will make.

Of course, a simple, almost primitive, view will insist that the unfortunate consequence of technological innovation is that it encourages only "aggressors" to pursue their evil designs. Experience might have taught us, however, that technology may tempt not only aggressors but the victims of aggression as well. The latter are not somehow provided with a natural immunity from the temptations posed by technology. They are not exempt from the temptation to assume that technological advance must always work to their advantage, presumably because they are the more virtuous. Nor have they been free from the temptation to entertain radical solutions to the security problem or from justifying these solutions by the claim that their purposes in employing technology are purely defensive in character. By a "logic" that is as recurring as the history of conflict, the potential victims of aggression may thus become in turn the potential aggressors. This "logic" is ultimately independent of technology, but technology may give it considerable stimulus and make its avoidance increasingly difficult.

If a temptation to seek radical solutions to the security problem has indeed become increasingly compelling, it is not simply because men have suddenly become morally irresponsible. There is something patently absurd in the complaint that a threat of extermination, even when restricted to preventing one's own annihilation, signifies a moral decline for which there is no explanation other than that men have deliberately chosen to abandon any sense of restraint. If men presently show less restraint in threatening their adversaries, it is largely because they are less secure than in an earlier age. Instruments whose very existence gives rise to this pervading sense of insecurity also give impetus to deep-rooted desires for radical solutions by providing these desires with an apparent plausibility. Moreover, the new technology, while profoundly aggravating men's sense of insecurity, has destroyed the margin men formerly enjoyed to correct the excesses bred by insecurity and to remedy an ill-chosen course of action. The most significant element providing this margin was time itself. Although collectives have threatened one another with annihilation before, the difficulties generally encountered in carrying out this threat have required time to overcome. Men could have time for second thoughts, time to contemplate the consequences of their actions as they saw those consequences unfold, time in which to turn back because of sheer exhaustion if not from a sense of horror and dismay over the excesses they had committed. In doing away with the difficulties formerly encountered in carrying out a threat virtually encompassing the enemy's annihilation, technology has also done away with the time required to carry out that threat. Time may no longer save men from the final excess, save them almost against their will. Instead of making them appear better than they were it may make them appear worse than they ever intended to be.

Index

Acheson, Dean: 5, 12, 25, 45, 46; on American purposes, 55; on basic premise of American policy, 17; on interpretation of armed attack, 41; on objectives in Korean war, 62; on peace through deterrence, 65-66; on preventive war, 15; on relationship of peace and justice, 30; on Soviet fears, 56

Aggression: dispute over definition of, 126 n.; indirect, 42, 47, 48, 51-52, 125, 138; interpretation of, 25-26; policy of containment and, 38-42; prevention of, 27-29, 65-68, 183-184; United Nations General Assembly as interpreter of, 44-53

American interpretation of international conflict: aggression in, 25-26, 183-184; containment and, 35-39; deterrence, philosophy of, and, 22-23; identification of aggressor in, 26-27; parallel between domestic and international society in, 27-29; preventive war rejected by, 24; voluntarism marking, 18-21, 183; war an unnecessary evil in, 23-24

American just war doctrine: ambivalence of, 21-23; causes of war and, 11-13; causes and objectives of war related in, 60-61; consensus marking, 6-7; defensive purposes avowed by, 54-56; deterrence and defense equated in, 65-66; ideological function of, 43; manner of employing force and, 74-93 *passim.;* neutrality and, 84 n.; notion of aggressor in, 25-26; nuclear technology and, 33-34; objectives undefined by, 74; peace and justice, relationship of, in, 30-33; policy of containment and, 35-40; preventive war condemned by, 14-18, 105; punitive character of, 72-73; reason of state contrasted with, 19-20; resort to war, justification for, in, 11-14; simplicity of, 11-14; unconditional surrender related to, 61; United Nations Charter and, 30-54 *passim;* voluntarism marking, 19-21

Armed attack, interpretation of, 41-42

B-36 bomber program, hearings on, 59

Bacon, Francis, 116

Balance of power: containment and, 36, 46; preventive war and, 116-118

Baldwin, Hanson, 108

Bellum justum, doctrine of, 128 n.

Berlin, 48-49, 186-187

Bowett, D. W., 127 n.

Bradley, Omar, 24, 59 n.

Brodie, Bernard, 106 n., 139 n., 143 n.

Butterfield, Herbert, 82 n., 158 n.

Chinese Communists, 186

War, renounced as instrument of national policy, 12-14, 34
Whelan, Joseph G., 39 n.
Williams, William A., 25 n.
Wilson, Woodrow, 12

Wolfers, Arnold, 102
World Council of Churches: on prevention of war in atomic age, 153-154 n.; on right of national self-defense, 155 n.